The Story of Bob

The Story of Bob

The Life and Times of the Rev. Robert W. Wood

Steven C. Law

with a foreword by
J. Bennett Guess

United Church Press
(an imprint of The Pilgrim Press)
1300 East 9th Street
Cleveland, Ohio 44114

thepilgrimpress.com

Published 2026.

Printed on acid-free paper.

Library of Congress Cataloging-in-Publication Data on file.
LCCN: 2025941415

ISBN (paper): 978-0-8298-2920-4
ISBN (ebook): 978-0-8298-2921-1

Printed in The United States of America.

For Donald

Love never ends.

—1 Corinthians 13:8

Foreword

I picked up the ringing phone in my Cleveland office. It was the Rev. Robert Watson Wood calling from his home in New Hampshire. The year was 2005, and I was editor of *United Church News*, the United Church of Christ's national print and online newspaper.

At the time, the UCC was invested in a multi-million-dollar branding campaign, seeking to define more clearly the denomination's public identity as a radically welcoming church. "Jesus didn't turn people away. Neither do we," the thirty-second TV spots proclaimed. The UCC also began heavily touting its long history of arriving early on issues of justice and inclusion.

Rev. Wood, at age eighty-two and long retired from his thirty-six years of pastoral ministry, introduced himself to me as the author of the pioneering 1960 book *Christ and the Homosexual.* Perhaps because of all the attention being paid to the UCC's historic "firsts," he bluntly criticized that his trailblazing contributions to advancing LGBTQ inclusion in church and society had been largely under-recognized and under-celebrated.

That was the first time I had ever heard of Bob Wood, I'm embarrassed now to admit. The unscheduled phone call lasted a long time, and I remember feeling emotionally exhausted by the time we hung up. Bob was passionate, driven, and intense, but his life story left quite an impression. We would speak a few more times after that.

Fast forward two decades, and more than seven years after Bob's death at the age of ninety-five in 2018, the publication of this stirring memoir is making things right.

More than forty years separated Bob Wood's life and ministry from my own, but I readily identify with so much that *The Story of Bob* explores: wanting to be a good little boy; possessing a vocation-shaping fascination with inclusive faith and justice advocacy; experiencing sexual adolescence and gay arousal through conflicting, confusing clues and experiences; being on the receiving end of taunts and ridicule; wishing and praying to be different; ultimately claiming the inherent dignity and self-worth that the church itself had planted; and above all, wanting others to learn, know, and live in that liberation, too. To simply trust in the *goodness* of the good news—can't we all just do that?

To be clear, I played no role in getting this book researched, written, or published, but having the honor of writing its foreword feels like a true full-circle moment. Because Bob was right, and as you read the pages that follow, you will be heartstruck time and time again by the immense courage, resolve, and integrity that flowed from this man's faith and character.

Each chapter, told in Bob's first-person voice, is the result of years of recorded interviews conducted by author Steven C. Law, who has beautifully captured and curated these reflections for us.

You'll feel the tensions and ambiguities of Bob's desire to live an authentic life at a time when society placed little to no value on such honesty. You'll see how he pushed against entrenched norms and assumptions, even as he walked the pragmatic tightropes essential to his own safety and survival. You'll be touched by the extreme thought and care he gave to being true to his values, especially in the details.

You'll marvel at his early involvement in the Mattachine Society, a decade before Stonewall, and his willingness to use his real name, clergy title, and photo when speaking up for gay rights. You'll find yourself swept up in his long medical recovery and deep introspection after taking a bullet to the chest during the Second World War.

You'll identify with his loving but complicated, ever-evolving relationships with his parents and brother; his longtime lover and spouse; his congregants and denominational leaders; even gay friends and his sexual trysts. You'll cry at all the love, the loss, the hard and beautiful discoveries.

Mostly, you'll find yourself forgetting just how darn early Bob Wood arrived on *everything*, even conceiving of, and advocating for, same-sex marriage some fifty or sixty years before the rest of us. *The Story of Bob* is strangely contemporary and relatable.

Rev. Wood starkly tells it like it was: how he found himself, his sexuality, his calling, and his ministry of authentic truth-telling, all in an era perfectly ill-prepared to offer him any support. Instead, he built his own framework of support, complete with a well-constructed theology and honed pastoral skills, work-life balance, self-care practices, and prayers and rituals to aid his search for meaning in it all.

Bob Wood is a name that LGBTQ people and our allies, especially open and affirming Christians and faith-based justice advocates, should recall with immense gratitude and pride.

At his core, Bob felt a high calling and sacred duty to end the hurt and resist the injury that have been inflicted upon LGBTQ people for centuries. He pushed back against spiritual violence long before that psychological concept existed. Bob knew that LGBTQ people were literally dying under the weight of society's ignorance and the church's ignoble complacency.

In fact, Bob's eagerness to confront those who weaponized scripture is what drove him to seminary in the first place. As he told the Oberlin LGBT History Project in 2000, he wanted "to learn my Bible as well as, or more than they did, so I could use scripture to confront them."

One of my favorite finger-snap moments in this book describes when Bob found himself part of an undergraduate pre-theology discussion group. The other students began to call into question Bob's salvation bonafides after he insinuated that believing Jesus literally walked on water needn't be a central tenet of the faith.

"The story depicts Jesus risking his own life to show concern for his friends," he schooled them, challenging their obsession on clearly the wrong thing. "Walking on water is not as important as Jesus's caring."

Amazingly, this episode happened in the 1940s, even before Bob had entered seminary. Almost instinctively at a young age, he rejected faith that instilled fear in place of more sorely needed love, compassion, and justice. His moral clarity was nearly pitch perfect. (Spoiler alert: a fed-up Bob henceforth stopped attending any more undergrad pre-theology meetings.)

In the UCC, we often tout our historic "firsts"—the first predominately white mainline church in the United States to ordain an African-American pastor (Lemuel Haynes, 1785);

the first woman pastor (Antoinette Brown, 1853); and the first openly gay pastor (William R. Johnson, 1972).

But the trouble with naming and claiming "firsts," as important as these distinctions can be, is that we're often left with an oversimplification of history. The truth is that few people, even the most celebrated few, truly showed up all by themselves. Others led or accompanied or encouraged them, mostly without recognition, to that threshold.

We forget that even our most celebrated trailblazers had trailblazers before them, courageous predecessors who tilled the hard ground—in their own unique and profound ways—so that all the good seeds of bravery that followed, whenever and wherever scattered, might find fertile soil to take root and grow.

The life, ministry, and legacy of the Rev. Robert Watson Wood is one of those remarkable antecedents that we do well to document and recount with the publishing of this moving volume. I am immensely grateful for Steven C. Law's research and writing perseverance that now ensures Bob's story will become forever part of our own.

The Rev. Dr. J. Bennett Guess, executive director of the American Civil Liberties Union of Ohio and former executive minister and national officer of the United Church of Christ

Preface

Does anyone ever feel completely at home in the family of human beings? If so, what is the path that leads there? How does one know?

And how does one measure their impact on the world as a historic figure?

Rev. Robert Watson Wood (Bob) was from "the greatest generation." He served in the Italian theater in the Second World War, was wounded, and spent twenty-two months recovering in military hospitals. During this time, he received a Combat Infantry Badge, a Bronze Star, two Battle Stars, and a Purple Heart. Feeling guilty having survived when so many of his comrades-in-arms had died, Bob felt the only meaningful thing to do with his life was to serve God, and that's what he did. He served as a United Church of Christ pastor for thirty-six years.

Bob was also a gay man. As a soldier, he had been asked to make the ultimate sacrifice in an institution with the stated policy that soldiers thought to be homosexual (the nomenclature of the time) would receive a dishonorable discharge and lose all veterans benefits. As a pastor he was a committed working professional in a world that espoused loving concern for all, yet he felt he couldn't be candid about his sexuality without jeopardizing his livelihood. Consequently, he lived a bifurcated life, never knowing when, where, or how to be himself fully.

He was ordained in 1951, when the church insisted that homosexuality was a sin and had no ministries for them; when Joseph McCarthy was stirring up hatred toward them; when the psychological community considered their lifestyle a mental disorder; and laws made it a crime. Despite these real and present challenges and dangers, through his ministry, Rev. Wood found a way to encourage a fuller life for the LGBTQ+ community.

Very early in his ministries, on his own time, he began to make notes for a book that took several years to write. *Christ and the Homosexual* was published in 1960, nine years before Stonewall. Rev. Wood's name was on its cover and title page. Back then, the few who wrote about such matters preferred pseudonyms. In his book, Bob described the homosexual community as he had come to know it, as well as their positive contributions to society. He was critical of the church. "When a church member or religious leader claims that homosexuality is a sin, they attack the sacredness of human personality," he wrote. He asserted that believing homosexuals were Christians. He encouraged Biblical scholars to rethink the scriptures interpreted as condemning homosexuality, called for a lifting of the ban against gays in the military, and expressed his willingness to perform same-sex marriages.

For the next decade, as time from his parish ministries permitted, he spoke and wrote publicly about his forward-thinking ideas.

He became an activist. On June 25, 1965, he was the only clergy person among twenty-four picketing the Federal Service Commission (FSC) Headquarters in Washington, DC, the first protest for gay rights in this country. The picket had been organized to protest the FSC policy of not hiring people thought to be homosexuals.

Within the church, he challenged the Board for Homeland Ministries (BHM)—the United Church of Christ instrumentality tasked with responding to justice issues: racism, women's equality, economic justice, poverty, etc.—to learn about the needs of homosexuals and development ministries for them. He gave the keynote address at the First National Conference on Religion and the Homosexual, portions of which were published in the *New York Times*, *Washington Post*, *Time* magazine, *Ladies Home Journal*, and others. He has been honored within his denomination and within society at large for being a pioneer in the gay rights movement in America. On August 18, 2018, his obituary in the *New York Times* featured the headline, "Robert Wood, 95, Dies; Urged Christian Acceptance of Gay People." Such effort and accomplishment did little to solve for him the puzzle of family and home, a subject of great importance to Bob.

Finding love and intimacy as a lifelong joy is difficult for many, regardless of sexual orientation. Bob's quest to find a life partner in those days was not easy and required risky behavior until he met Hugh Macmaster Coulter, a rodeo cowboy/artist, in a bar in Manhattan. The two men fell in love. One night, they had a private, unofficial wedding ceremony in the church parsonage in which they exchanged rings and vows. They supported each other in their careers, through family crises, and ill health. They traveled together. Although deep love and affection was exchanged between these two men, they never shared a home together. Fear.

After his retirement from Christian ministry, Bob moved from Maynard, Massachusetts, to Concord, New Hampshire while Hugh remained in Pepperell, Massachusetts. Bob and Hugh began to make plans to live under the same roof for the first time in their life. They were formalizing these plans when Bob visited Hugh in 1989. On January 3, Bob awoke before Hugh, as was their pattern, and went down to make breakfast. When he called for Hugh to come down, there was no answer. When he went back upstairs, he discovered that Hugh had died in his sleep. He knelt beside the bed, said a prayer, then made a call to the police—a courageous act, given the time and place.

When the police arrived and questioned Bob about who he was and why he was in Hugh's house, after their twenty-six years together, all Bob could say was, "I'm Mr. Coulter's pastor."

He planned Hugh's funeral. Parishioners from Bob's churches attended the funeral. Afterward, one well-meaning parishioner came up to say, "I'm sorry about the loss of your friend."

"He wasn't just my friend," Bob said through tears, "he was my lover."

At sixty-six, Bob was alone in his grief. In the weeks and months that followed, he began to feel emotionally drained, sad, and empty. Having read about Hugh's passing, I reached out to Bob to offer my condolences. Soon after, I visited him as a pastor would visit someone in grief.

Bob spoke exclusively about Hugh and how much he missed him. On subsequent visits, I began to wonder if the details of Bob's life merited a book, so I requested time to discover the story. Luckily, Bob was a keeper of letters, sermons, speeches, war diaries, and many personal documents now held at the Congregational Library in Boston. He provided a list of people with whom I might speak to understand his life and accomplishments more fully. These interviews helped guide my conversations with him and eventually led to chapters organized around moments that held emotional weight. Bob himself was emotionally shut down and had difficulty naming or expressing feelings. When we reviewed chapters, I asked him to read them aloud with a concern for accuracy of facts and emotions. When reading my rendering of his emotions, he often wept. Over time I came to believe that his story deserved to be written for both historical and personal reasons.

During the five years it took to research and write the book, I discovered that few people, including his family, knew of his love for Hugh. Bob sought to correct this. He came out to his local church, then to his brother. He allowed *Out* magazine to publish his photo in a photo essay on pioneers of the Gay Rights Movement. He agreed to be interviewed for a documentary on the same subject. Articles about him appeared in the *Advocate*, *Boston's Gay Community News*, and the *Concord Monitor*, to name a few. He helped facilitate inclusive policies at the Havenwood-Heritage Heights Retirement Community where he lived. He began speaking to church groups, including an annual interfaith Holocaust service in which he led a remembrance of the half million "pink triangle men" killed with the Jews in Nazi concentration camps. Most importantly, he found ways to publicly acknowledge his relationship with Hugh.

Readers curious about a life of faith will discover a personal evolution of ideas. Liberation theologians will recognize such details as praxis, the way faith is lived. Through Sunday school lessons, a prayer sent by a mother to a son going to war, studies in seminary, answers to complex questions by parishioners, or individual Bible verses that inform an emotional state or traditions that inspire risk-taking on behalf of an oppressed group, faith is an ever-present reality that helped Bob survive difficult times, even ones brought about in the name of faith. That same faith led Bob to second-guess his decision to live apart from Hugh, recalling moments when they had stopped an impulse to hold hands or kiss so as not to offend. He felt deep regret about those missed moments of shared affection and prayed for forgiveness. He meditated on 1 John 4:18: "There is no fear in love, but perfect love casts out fear." Such can only be experienced in hindsight. Forgiven, liberated, he now wanted the whole world to know about his love for Hugh and hoped that my book about his life might achieve that goal.

Recent political and religious messaging reminds me of the forties and fifties. Just like then, moralistic puritan reasoning based on literal interpretations of the Bible would have LGBTQ+ folks think of themselves as sinful or sick. Bigoted people can seldom be persuaded to think differently. However, I hope this book will help others to think for themselves and form solidarity with Rev. Wood, a man of faith who sought love, justice, and inclusion for LGBTQ+ people, instead of judgment. We inhabit this world for such a short time, any idea that improves our character—helps us live and love fully and maximize our potential—is a good thing. My hope is that reading about Bob will inspire us to seek ways to love well and discover home.

Around the Radio

One Tuesday in 1928, my mother, Edith Watson (Beard) Wood, set up her ironing board, plugged in an electric flat iron, and filled a bowl with cool water in which she dipped her hand to sprinkle clothes to be ironed. She ironed on Tuesdays because she washed clothes on Mondays. She wore a cotton print housedress, a half apron, and low-heeled shoes. Surrounding her were piles of shirts, trousers, socks, underwear, and handkerchiefs belonging to my brother, Harold, Jr., my father, Harold Nelson Wood, Sr., and myself. I was five years old.

Harold was four years older and my most reliable playmate. He returned to school, leaving me a little lost and alone with

Mother. Seeing that I did not know what to do with myself, Mother encouraged me to go outside to play. To keep my good clothes clean, she had made a shortsleeved jump suit with roomy legs and pockets to rest my hands. I put on my jump suit and ran out our back door. Mother allowed me to roam and play within earshot of her voice.

Single-family, clapboard houses on stone foundations lined our street, the main thoroughfare through a new development in Youngstown, Ohio. Most of the houses had separate garages and lawns linked together by new sidewalks and backyards that became playgrounds at a moment's notice.

My playmates lined up outside a neighbor's garage, mimicking Skippy Skinner's Radio Show by creating secret passwords to gain admittance. Eventually, we all guessed the password and found ourselves inside the garage. Someone suggested we play *Renfrew of the Royal Mounted*, so we ran back outside where we pretended to be caught in howling storms, chased by wolves, or rescuing victims in distress.

Suddenly, one of the boys said, "Let's play cops and robbers." I ran in the house to grab my cap gun and holster. Mother, still ironing, told me to slow down as I scurried past her to rejoin my friends.

My playmates and I took turns being cops or robbers, being the chaser or being chased. When my turn came to be cop, I put on my pretend badge, took my cap gun out of its holster, and just like a hero in a Roy Roger Western, I arrested a robber who had been hiding behind a tree.

Without warning, Mother's voice interrupted our play. "Stop pointing that gun," she said. "You know the rules."

My brother and I knew the rules. We were not to play with the knobs on the Philco Radio in the living room: "Your father has it tuned, and you'll mess it up," Mother said repeatedly. We were to be courteous and quiet in the company of adults, unless spoken to. We were not to mistreat the family cat. When

Mother admonished me in front of my friends, I remembered the rule that prohibited pointing my toy gun at other children.

But I was full of myself and having fun. In front of the other children, I turned to her and defiantly said "no."

"Bobby, you get in the house this minute," she said. "Go to your room until your father gets home."

I pouted, frozen in place.

"Go on," she demanded. "Get in there. And the rest of you children go home."

I went to my room, feeling on the verge of a tantrum. I couldn't concentrate to read a book, nor did I wish to play with toys stored away in a toy box my father had built. I just stared at the wallpaper stars on my ceiling, wondering what my father would say. As usual he left for his job at Youngstown Electric at 7:30 that morning. He would return at 5:30.

After a while I heard Mother downstairs putting the ironing board away. I listened as she walked back and forth from our Westinghouse refrigerator to a cutting board. I heard the rattling of pots and pans. She would have her cookbook opened on the kitchen counter. I smelled onions and ham cooking and heard water running in the sink. The screen door slammed—my brother coming in from school. Chair legs scraped the kitchen floor. He was getting milk and cookies, I thought. I would have been eating cookies too had I not been confined to my room. After two hours I heard Father's car pull into the driveway. The back door opened. I imagined him hanging his fedora on the hat rack before disappearing to change out of his blue suit, tie, and crisp, starched, white shirt. He'd take off his shined black leather shoes and put his pocketwatch on the bureau.

Normally we would play together before supper, but not today. I felt queasy and apprehensive about what might happen next.

"Wash your hands for dinner, Bobby," Mother called. I obeyed and joined my family around the table.

After grace, followed by minutes of silence, finally my father spoke.

"Mother tells me you've been a bad boy," he said. "You pointed a gun at a playmate and talked back to her when she told you to come into the house. This is serious. What do you think we should do?"

No doubt my brother enjoyed this scolding. However, he stayed quiet, looking at my father then at me then back at my father then back at me, while Mother quietly served our plates. I lowered my head and played with my ham-and-bean casserole.

"I asked you a question," Father said abruptly.

"I don't know," I replied.

"I think you should go to bed early and when you say your prayers, ask God to make you a good boy."

Good boys, according to my parents, attended the Evergreen Presbyterian Church—a large, yellow brick building where we went to worship God. A small orchestra accompanied the choir there. The joyous and serious sounds of music entertained me, but the preaching escaped my understanding.

What I learned about God was taught to me in Sunday School and at home. Jesus loves little children and people of all skin colors; Jesus is God's love; God loves us by providing nice parents, our church building, schools, teachers, rain, sun, brothers, sisters, and everything good in our world. Potted plants growing on the windowsill illustrated God's activity in nature. Praying for others taught me to be less selfish, which God desired. I believed that God would take care of me "if" I was a good boy—stayed clean, acted nice, ate right, and obeyed adults. Disappointing my parents seemed tantamount to disappointing God. And nothing could disappoint my parents faster than willful disobedience.

After supper I returned to my bedroom and cried as darkness engulfed the room. Streetlights projected eerie reflections of branches on the walls. Knowing how to find the light switch kept me from feeling afraid.

Downstairs, my parents and brother listened to Lowell Thomas on the radio. I imagined my father relaxing in his favorite chair, wearing his smoking jacket, reading his newspaper, smoking a cigarette, flipping ashes into the floor stand ashtray, and cracking jokes and laughing. Mother would be sitting with her mending or sewing.

I hugged my Teddy Bear, which in that moment felt like my only friend. On the one hand, my parents' loving ways helped me feel secure. They bragged about my grade school poems and drawings, lemonade stands, good report cards, or cookies I baked. They asked questions: "What did you do today? Where did you go? What did you see?" Their interest in me was a source of constant affirmation. I couldn't have wished for a better childhood—the love of my parents and the security of home—an idyllic state I would have done anything to protect and certainly would have avoided doing anything to jeopardize. But lying alone in my room, in that well-ordered, predictable childhood environment, with its rhythms and routines, rules and moral definitions, love felt conditional. God, too, seemed remote, almost nonexistent.

I heard intermittent laughter throughout the evening: "Jack Benny" and "Fibber McGee and Mollie." There would be no card games or "Button, Button, Who's Got the Button" that night.

Mother eventually came in.

"Bobby, would you like me to read you a bedtime story?"

"Yes."

"Have you learned your lesson?"

"Yes."

Mother began to read. My shame and sadness melted into her words and finally into her arms, where I cried again.

An Experience of God

On my twelfth birthday, in May 1935, a teacher asked the students in my class what frightened them. Classmates shouted out snakes, the boogieman, and ghosts.

"Not having enough time," I said, strangely.

Maybe I was thinking about Harold. He left home for the New York Military Academy the previous September. Through letters and visits back home, I knew he was alive and well. Although glad not to have to compete with him for my parents' attention and affection, I missed playing together, hearing his stories about school, and his companionship on family outings and at home.

Later that day, at dusk, having opened presents and eaten cake and ice cream with my parents, I was drawn to my brother's old bedroom, where a shaft of light from an unseen source illuminated his bed. Amazed and bewildered by the light, I fixed my eyes on it, wondering if it might be from God.

I had been reading the Bible on my own. My grandmother, Mary Beard, encouraged the habit, saying, "You're old enough to read, and the Lord wrote the Bible in English so you could." I memorized the Beatitudes, the Ten Commandments, and Psalm 23, quoting them before the congregation at church, accomplishments for which I received considerable praise. Bible lessons conveyed right living and pointed me toward how I most wanted to be. Reading the Bible had given me a new sense of mystery. God was in the Bible and my awareness of God was growing, especially in confirmation classes.

My confirmation teacher defined Pentecost as God sending the Holy Spirit to guide the disciples after Jesus' crucifixion. He spoke of salvation, God's desire for us to experience rebirth and new life. He taught us about stewardship and our responsibility to give something back to God.

"God wants to be your friend," he said over and over. For the first time I felt included in God's plans. Through my prayers I welcomed God as my friend.

I fell to my knees beside my brother's bed, and closed my eyes to pray:

"Thank you, God, for my twelve years," I said. "They have passed so quickly. I still have so many things to do. Could you let me live ninety more years?"

A warm feeling of two-way communication came over me. God had answered my prayers. I believed that God granted my desire to remain alive for ninety more years. When I opened my eyes, the shaft of light was gone. However, left behind was the strong feeling that God cared about me personally.

An Object of Fantasy

In 1937, as a fourteen-year-old, I attended Camp Stanbaugh, where my fellow Boy Scouts and I hiked, studied nature, created crafts, swam, and canoed to advance to become Eagle Scouts. In our free time we played Capture the Flag, went on scavenger hunts, and wrestled Roman style. We pushed, shoved, yelled, and ran throughout the day, but soon after dusk we settled into our bunks.

Lean-tos, cabins, tepees, tree houses, and grass huts were built on hills along nature trails through the woods and beside lakes. Along the waterfront I slept in a cabin with nine scouts and a counselor.

One night, after we had settled into our bunks, our counselor lectured us.

"Girls are different from boys," he said. "You're supposed to be nice to girls. But you go to bed with them only after you're married, and you never stick your penis into a girl until you want a baby."

That word *penis* had us howling.

"And, if you are morally straight, you don't play around with it, no rubbing; it's just for number one, and you certainly don't touch each other's."

I blushed, wondering what he meant, hoping someone would ask him to explain, but no one dared to question the counselor. The serious tone of his voice did not invite questions.

The next day, in a shower room by the lake, a fellow scout and I changed out of our wet bathing suits. "You're not supposed to touch it," he said to me, laughing.

"You can touch mine if I can touch yours."

"Let's." I touched. He touched. We were mocking the counselor's lecture.

Later, on a hot, still, muggy summer night I feigned sleep. The heat and humidity had me sweating in my bunk when one of my bunkmates, wearing only his moccasins, got up, a flashlight in hand, to go to the latrine. Curious to see his nude body, I remained awake to watch him return. But he remained hidden in darkness behind a swirling beam of light. Briefly, I caught a glimpse of moonlight reflecting on his back and rear. I was aware that I was looking and feeling a new kind of pleasure.

On the last Friday night of camp, our parents sat on logs encircling an arena in the center of which blazed a fire, casting a glow on the trees overhead. Counselors organized Scouts into pretend Cowboys or Indians.

"Wood, you're an Indian," my counselor commanded. "Indians, strip down to your shorts and form a line to paint up."

We did so. Before us were pots of paint on a wooden table. A boy to my left stuck a finger into red paint. Two quick swipes across his forehead left behind two red stripes. He dipped again into blue paint and made a streak down his nose. I began to paint my body, first bright green, making circles around my nipples, then dark blue, making squiggly snakes down the middle of my stomach and polka dots along my arms and cheeks. Smearing the paint sent chills over my skin.

"Take off your shorts and underwear, too, and put these on," the counselor commanded, handing us a swath of flimsy cloth—dark green cotton. "Go behind the bushes. Pretend it's a diaper. Pull the cloth tight between your legs. Secure it around your waist with your belt, and let the flaps hang over."

Cowboys entered the arena first. On cue, Indians attacked. I yelled, danced up and down, shouted war cries, knocked cowboys over, until one pointed his cap gun at me and shot. I clutched my chest, doubled over, screamed my loudest scream, and fell to the ground. Against the cool, dusty earth, I felt myself becoming erect. Boys in loincloths continued to dance all around me.

Back in my cabin I wrapped the cloth in a clean towel and stuffed it into the bottom of my footlocker until the following day when I packed it to bring home. I hid the cloth in the back of one of my dresser drawers but later, thinking my mother might find it, I stuffed it into one of my Sunday shoes. I never concealed anything from my parents before.

That night, I smuggled the cloth into bed before Mother came in to kiss me good night. After my prayers I pulled off my pajama bottoms, draped the loincloth between my legs, pulled it up as tight as I could, and tried to recreate the feeling I had felt lying in the dirt at camp. I recalled the nude boy in moonlight and the boys dancing in a circle. Soon I felt my penis become erect, and that was another pleasure. I made no association between the cloth and my parents' rules. However, I was somehow certain they would have disapproved.

That cloth remained an object of fantasy for me well into the fall when Dad took a new job for the electric company in Lorain, Ohio, just west of Cleveland along Lake Erie.

Adolescence

In Lorain I joined a Scout troop. My parents transferred our church memberships from the Evergreen Presbyterian to the First Congregational, which was the church closest to our new home. At Lorain High School I nearly made straight A's on my first report card, the one exception being a C in Latin.

Jean Gard and I both struggled with Latin. Jean's mother, who had taught Latin, offered to tutor us. So twice a week I walked to her house. After each lesson Jean and I talked. We discovered we shared interests in music and movies. At school we often met for lunch and after school I often invited her to a soda shop. We became friends. For our first date I invited her to an Andy Hardy movie.

My role model for how to be a teenager was Mickey Rooney's character Andy Hardy. His actions always led to a crisis—broken windows or a wrecked family car. To help solve his problems, Hardy sought help from neighbors, a police officer, or a clergyman. Usually, he had a faithful, steady girlfriend throughout the crisis. Jean stood by me in a comparable way.

I escorted Jean to parties at friends' houses and school functions so often that our schoolmates expected to see us together. Soon, we were "going steady," which I understood to mean that we would be true to each other and wouldn't date others.

Although I knew that other couples necked or madeout, I was too shy to relate to Jean in such a physical way. Our friends noticed. Once, at a beach party, our friends intentionally left us alone. They returned, teasing us that we were no closer than when they had left.

"I am willing to wait," Jean responded virtuously.

"Me too," I said, unsure what I was waiting for.

I never dreamed about Jean or thought about her in sexual ways. All I needed or wanted from her was friendship. I dated her because I liked her, and she liked me.

My sexual feelings happened in isolated and stupid ways. There were no talk shows, support groups, or public education campaigns about sex back then, and I couldn't discuss sex with my parents. Nice people didn't talk about such things. I learned about sex over time through conflicting, confusing clues, which remained unexamined. However, I can honestly say that these feelings came naturally to me. I didn't plan to have them.

Once, I felt a physical attraction to a basketball player on our school team. Another time, a classmate wearing tights in his role as Sir Walter Raleigh in a class drama caught my attention. I enjoyed looking at these boys, and if I had been courageous enough, I might have touched them. But touching, I knew, would have consequences—being beaten up, told on, or ridiculed.

Once, three schoolmates and I left campus to eat lunch at a soda shop. On our way back to school we passed a swishy older man mincing down the opposite side of the street. The old man wore a floppy hat and a boutonniere in his lapel.

"He's probably a queer," one of my classmates said, laughing at the man's effeminate way of walking.

"Yeah, probably," the other boy said and laughed.

I laughed too, trying to be like my friends. I ridiculed to keep from being ridiculed. We talked about queers, but no one admitted to knowing one or knowing about what they did. I was curious to learn about them.

During my senior year I went to the public library on a school assignment. On a stand in the center of the library I opened the Unabridged Webster's Dictionary, which I assumed held every word in the English language. Peering around to make sure no one could sneak up on me, I looked up the word *homosexual*. There was a scientific-sounding sentence about having sex with the same sex, nothing about loincloths or fantasies.

Soon after I walked to a park beside an ice-skating rink. The beach house, concessions stand, and a dressing area, all closed for the winter, were bathed in late afternoon light. Picnic tables were stacked against the beach house. Newly fallen snow formed drifts against the tables. With a stick, I drew a giant penis in the snow but quickly erased it. Perhaps part of me, intuitively, understood that I was a homosexual without possessing a clear understanding of what, in fact, a homosexual was.

Dating Jean helped me believe that I was not a homosexual. We had been a couple for three years when we attended our high school senior prom, which had the theme "ships": friendship, fellowship, scholarship, and sportsmanship. As a host couple for the prom, Jean and I decorated the scholarship table in blue and gold crepe paper. To symbolize scholarship, we arranged a centerpiece of books, a globe, a ruler, a diploma, and a graduation cap and tassel.

We rode to the prom with another couple. Jean looked beautiful in her cream-colored flowing dress trimmed with sparkling beads and a string of imitation pearls, a blue sash, gold pumps, and the orchid corsage I bought her. I wore a navy-blue suit and tie. A band played 1940s tunes, and I danced with Jean throughout the night. If you didn't dance, people would think you were a wallflower.

We left the prom early to go to a movie. Jean and I rode in the back seat of our friend's car. After the movie, on our way home, we held hands. I'm sure Jean would have preferred a boy with whom she could cuddle instead of a stiff-postured boy holding her hand. She asked me if I loved her. I thought a minute and told her I didn't. She pulled away; I think she cried. I was too embarrassed to look at her.

"How was the dance?" Mother asked the next day.

"Everybody was there," I replied. "We danced together. The girls looked nice in their evening gowns."

"What movie did you see?" Father asked.

"*Gone with the Wind*."

"Did you like it?"

"It's a great war movie, with romance stuff. Jean asked me if I loved her and I said, 'no.'"

"That's probably the right answer," Mother said. "You're too young to get too attached."

Mother's pardon did not remove the guilt I felt for having hurt another person.

After graduation, on my last visit to Jean's home, we exchanged presents. Jean gave me a five-year diary and I gave her a monogrammed leather briefcase. We had a pleasant visit. Upon leaving, Jean's mother turned to me.

"It is just as well you said 'no,'" she said. "Jean will be off to college in the fall, and I'm sure she will be popular with young men there. It's not the end of the world for either of you, just a new beginning."

"Yes, a new beginning," I replied. I felt relieved.

Leaving Home

After my high school graduation, Father retired from his job at Ohio Edison and our family moved from Lorain to Bomoseen, Vermont, several miles from Fair Haven, his hometown. His father had been a carpenter there, and houses he had built remained set apart by gingerbread details crafted during long winters two generations before. That summer, using building skills he learned from his father, Father oversaw the construction of a retirement home—a slate-roofed cape with a view of Bird's Eye Mountain.

That August, in the methodical way of an engineer, my father handed me a ledger listing the expenses I could expect at college as well as a schedule of payments that he would send to me.

"Good planning almost eliminates surprises," he said in his soft, reassuring voice. He explained each entry on his list.

I was eighteen. Six years in the Boy Scouts had prepared me to be an achiever. Good grades, acting, debating, and editing the yearbook had earned me enough graduation points to have my name inscribed on a bronze plaque at Lorain High School. Academically, I felt confident. Reading, English, and my work on the yearbook staff had motivated me to major in journalism at the University of Pennsylvania.

In September 1941, my parents drove me in their 1940 Ford to the train station in Whitehall, New York. Dad preferred big cars for their security, comfort, and safety. His head with a neat, short haircut held in place with Vitalis rose above the front seat in front of me. He smoked one of his Old Gold cigarettes. Mother sat silently beside him. Dressed in a sports jacket, shirt, and tie, I sat in the backseat with my new Underwood typewriter. We rolled out of our driveway past a new picket fence and an old gas light my father had electrified.

We rode down Old Route 4, past Coon's Store where I had worked that summer, along Lake Bomoseen by the summer cottages and hotels, then into Fair Haven past the First Congregational Church where my father's family had been members for generations. We attended church there during our summer vacations from Youngstown and Lorain.

"You'll be looking for a church near campus to attend?" Mother said as we passed the church.

"Yes," I said, thinking about Rev. Arthur Wells, Fair Haven's newest pastor, fresh out of seminary. My parents liked his preaching, and I welcomed his enthusiasm for young people. He shook my hand the Sunday before as he warned me about new and conflicting ideas I might learn in college before adding a warning that I must "keep the faith."

"I hope there's a Congregational Church near campus," I said.

Dad smiled and glanced at me through the rearview mirror. Mother turned around in her seat, half facing me.

"The denomination doesn't matter," she said, "the habit of attending does."

My father raised his eyebrows, and our eyes met again in the mirror. I thought he was going to crack a joke.

"Think twice about joining a fraternity, son," he said in a serious tone. "Don't be rushed into anything. Maybe you'll take your brother's suggestion and join the ROTC."

When he had been at home on furlough just weeks earlier, my brother, then a Second Lieutenant in the Army Transportation Corps, suggested I try out for the ROTC. Dressed in his uniform, he appeared self-confident, more like a friend to our father rather than me. I envied the rapport between them and felt jealous of the esteem my father granted him.

"And be sure to write Harold from time to time," Mother said.

"Yes," I said, "I will."

"Your brother had four good years at Penn," Father said. "We hope you can do as well."

"I'll do my best," I said.

We rode in silence for a while, and I looked out at the mountains with high pastures on which cattle grazed. When we arrived at the station, I carried my typewriter and my father's old tan, leather suitcase, which he had used to attend business meetings and conventions. Now that old suitcase, like a piece of my father's reliable nature, was going with me into my new world.

I wondered who would help Mother with her housework now that I was leaving and how my father would adjust to being retired. Looking at them, quiet now, waiting to send off their youngest child, I began to reflect on the ways they had protected me. If they had marital problems, they hadn't shown them. If they had economic troubles, they would never let on, even through the Great Depression. They protected my brother and me from any concern of financial hardship.

My train steamed in. Mother hugged and kissed me.

"We pray you have a safe trip, son," she said. "Be a good student, now. We're so proud. God bless you."

I looked at her face, which bore the emotions for our entire family, and hugged her.

My father stoically shook my hand, leaving a ten-dollar bill behind.

"You're on your own, son," while patting me on the back. "When we see you at Christmas, you'll be a real college student."

Mother handed me a box of cookies to eat on the train. I boarded and sat next to a window. The train began to roll, and we waved to each other. I leaned against the window and watched their waving hands grow smaller, until my father led Mother by the arm back into the station. For a while, I felt sadness seeing them disappear in the distance, but gradually the sadness became excitement. I was glad to be on my way, separated from my parents, free. I'll be a good student, I thought, and show them that I deserve their confidence in me.

ALONE

Outside the train station, I hailed a taxi. Philadelphia was larger than any city I had ever seen. Cars, buses, and trolleys bustled. Pedestrians ambled along sidewalks and crosswalks. Excited by the sights and sounds, I gawked along the way, hoping we were headed in the right direction. Soon the taxi driver pointed out the university dormitories.

Tudor-style buildings, looking like the Ivy League or even Oxford, surrounded the quadrangle. The architecture made me feel I was soon to be immersed in a stable historical old order.

Furnished with a bed, bureau, desk, and a straight back chair, my dorm room overlooked a botanical garden. The trees, shrubs, birds, and evergreens connected me, as they had at home, to the natural order described in my Sunday school lessons. My father, hoping to minimize distractions while I studied, agreed to pay the extra cost of a private dorm room. I could come and go as I pleased: no reports, no explanations.

Eager to maximize the opportunity before me, I attended every class lecture. After English classes, reading and writing assignments kept me in the library or in my dorm room. My efforts paid off in good grades, which pleased my father, who kept reminding me in telephone conversations, "I'm not paying for you to have fun and make friends, I'm paying for you to learn."

He need not have worried: when it came to friendships, I floundered. There were 600 students in my college class, compared to sixty in high school. There were so many people to get to know. I felt overwhelmed.

I tried to enroll in the Army ROTC but failed the physical because of a hernia, a surprise to me, my parents, as well as our family physician in Vermont.

When I attended the Presbyterian Church near campus, no one asked me about myself, and I didn't volunteer any information. I listened to the sermons, sang hymns, left my offerings, and departed quickly.

University policy required first-year students to participate in sports, so I chose fencing. I traveled with my teammates to tournaments at other colleges. We slept in dorm rooms, and horsed around after dark, throwing pillows and pulling off each other's blankets. When others bragged about their sexual experiences, I remained within myself, quiet and apart.

I ate my meals and walked to classes with my fellow classmates from Warwick dorm. We even helped each other with homework. At night I ambled down the hallway, looking for an open door where students sat around and talked. Topics of conversations floated from professors and fraternities to girls. Someone, it seemed, was always talking about girls.

One night a group of us went to a strip club where smoke and hucksters' calls filled the air.

Girls in feathers, sequins, wide-brim hats, long gloves, trailing fur pieces, satin gowns, boots to the knees, and costume jewelry came onto the stage, one by one.

"Take it off. Take it off," the audience yelled.

And the girls took it off, one piece at a time, down to their rhinestone G-strings and pasties, before disappearing off stage. Each girl then peeked around a side curtain and, with a wink, tossed her G-string onto the stage. This final act always made the men roar.

My classmates knew the strippers by name. They seemed pleased with themselves. They pranced around like young roosters, shouting and posturing. I was bored. The girls didn't do a thing for me. The only men in the show were clowns wearing baggy pants.

Gradually, I stopped seeking companionship with fellow classmates. Occasionally, I began to venture downtown alone, walking around, feeling anonymous, lost in a pleasant way.

The trolley tracks from campus to downtown were elevated for a few blocks, making them level with second story windows on houses across the street. Once, I saw lamps lighting a nude man through pulled-down shades. That night, back in my dorm room, I fantasized about him.

Another time I rode to Penn Station. I enjoyed the station's grand architecture and the waiting rooms, and watching strangers check chalked-in schedules for train platforms and arrival and departure times. I remember the men's room there: the antiseptic smell, the Black attendant sweeping the tile floor, the twenty sinks and toilet compartments, and a whole wall of white urinals. Men dressed casually or in military uniforms or business suits came and went, many in a hurry to catch trains, others lingering and looking around.

Pretending to wash my hands at the sink, I anxiously watched the urinals on the other side of the room. A man stared at me, and I looked in another direction. I dried my hands before surveying the stalls to see if they were occupied: I looked for feet. I returned to the mirror, scared and stimulated. I stared in the mirror, combed my hair, and stole glances at the men standing at the urinals, and waited. I could see them looking at each other, watching over their shoulders to see who was coming into the room. I didn't know for sure why I was there and refused consciously to admit to myself the obvious reason. But being there felt electric, my whole body alive, sensitive to touch, longing for release, yet fearful at the same time. I stored up sights to relive them in fantasy back in my room.

Months went by before these physical impulses drew me downtown again, this time to see a movie at the Mastabaum Theater. The restroom there was in the basement. The foyer was decorated with plush seats and couches, an artificial fireplace, and tapestries. Men came and went, entering and leaving the bathroom. Again, some lingered and smoked. I watched, like a voyeur of sorts: more fantasy. Men in military uniforms garnered attention from older men baiting them with lines that sounded like the movies such as "want a cigarette, sailor? Need a place to stay overnight?" No one ever approached me. I would have been embarrassed.

Weeks, even months, would go by with no sexual stimulation to speak of, but eventually, lured by sexual curiosity, I would travel back to these public restrooms. I didn't know where else to go. I feared going and while there I felt nervous to the point of distraction. I calmed down when I returned to campus, the security of my room, and the schedule of college life.

Pearl Harbor

After church on December 7, 1941, while in my room writing a letter to my parents, one of my dorm mates came running down the hall.

"War! War! War! The Japanese are bombing us," he yelled.

Students gathered in his room around a highpowered radio transmitting reports from Hawaii. The news sounded fragmented; the radio transmissions filled with static. Sirens and explosions sounded in the background as a reporter conveyed the catastrophe of United States Naval ships being bombed by Japanese planes. The news of the surprise attack shocked us: we wondered how the Japanese could get through

America's defense systems. Hearing that American service members had died saddened me, and I worried for those still under attack. For the rest of the day, we were glued to the radio as reports, some predicated on rumor, came in from around the world.

One report described the bombing of America's West coast; another warned that Japanese ships and airplanes were approaching California. Still another report alleged that spies had infiltrated the United States and cautioned us against speaking to strangers. Reports from Pearl Harbor continued throughout the day. Casualty figures climbed as well as calculations about the number of ships and airplanes destroyed. Businesses closed. A declaration of war seemed imminent.

Some of my classmates began to talk about quitting school to enlist. I wanted to seek advice from my father, but the telephone lines were jammed.

That night, alone in my room, I heard a siren wail over the campus. Information about what to do during an air raid came over the radio. Along with others hearing the siren, I turned off my lights and walked outside. Trolleys stopped. Lights around the quadrangle went dark. Tudor structures so familiar to me during the day were barely visible. In that eerie moment, I felt the war come home. Then came a two-siren "all clear," and we gathered in each other's rooms for more radio news and talk. Everybody had opinions.

Later, back in my room, I knelt beside my bed.

"God, stop all this!" I prayed. "Help me to understand what's happening. Be with our boys in the military, particularly my brother, and with our leaders as they make decisions. Help me to know what to do. Don't let this be the end of the world."

I really thought it might be. I didn't sleep well that night.

The following Tuesday I attended a special meeting of the Christian Association, a campus organization for students with religious concerns. About a dozen students, including women (university classes were still segregated by gender), sat around a table. A chaplain opened our meeting with a question.

"So, what do you think about the president's declaration of war?"

We all talked at once with a flood of questions.

"How long do you think the war will last?"

"How can I find out about my brother in the Army?"

"What will happen to German and Japanese students on campus?"

"Should we be praying to win?"

"Let's get the facts first," the chaplain said calmly. "Not everything you hear on the radio or read in the newspaper is true—it might be propaganda. Not all Germans and Japanese are bad. Pray and think before you act. Keep your mind on your studies."

Soon, the university issued sand, buckets, shovels, and stirrup pumps for our dormitories. Air raid wardens began to coordinate blackout procedures. In special classes, students learned how to fight fires. We also learned that hallways were the safest place to be during an enemy bombing.

When I finally reached my father on the telephone, I mentioned how classmates had been talking about leaving school to enlist.

"What's the university's policy?" he asked, calmly.

I told him about the Military Enlisted Reserve Corps in which students could enlist, choose their branch of service, and continue in school until the military called them to report for active duty.

"That sounds reasonable," he said. "With any luck the war will be over before they need to call you up. Have you thought about what branch of service you would like to join?"

"Army," I said.

"That's where your brother is, and I was," he replied. "We're Army people you know."

Army people, I thought: a great grandfather in the Civil War, a father in the First World War, now my brother, somewhere in the United States waiting to go to war, and me.

The following week I walked across campus to the armory that housed the College Recruitment Program office.

"What branch?" a bulldog officer barked from behind a desk.

"Army," I answered sheepishly.

"Over there." He pointed toward twenty men lined up before another officer sitting behind a desk. I joined the line.

From the sound of conversations around me, I realized that fellow students were in line. Others were Philadelphia residents. The line moved fast, and soon I faced the officer who scheduled an appointment for a physical, which I passed.

Two days later, with 200 other men, I held up my hand to take the oath of allegiance to the United States of America.

"Put us in uniform and give us six months and the war will be over," a man to my left said.

"One American can kill three Japs," someone else said.

"What do we need training for?" a man behind me said. "I know how to kill those bastards."

I was wondering what I was getting myself into. I was serious-minded, quiet, and reserved. I didn't want to hurt or kill anyone or die.

WAITING

After taking the oath, life continued with the knowledge that at any time orders might arrive that would change the predictable patterns of daily living. The winter cold and snow had begun, and I made plans to visit my folks for Christmas. Soon after, I noticed one of my fellow students touched a mezuzah hanging outside his door before entering his room. I asked if he had plans to go home for the holidays. He looked up from a book he was reading.

"I haven't a home anymore," he said. He explained how his family had to flee Germany because of Hitler. I felt sad for him but couldn't really fully comprehend his loss.

That weekend I took a train home, and my parents met me at the station. My father, who distrusted the news reports about Pearl Harbor, doubted we were getting the correct casualty figures. He even guessed that Roosevelt had somehow orchestrated the attack on Pearl Harbor to get us into a war. His strident tone took me by surprise.

"Let's not let all this talk about war spoil our Christmas," Mother said.

We stopped talking.

Days later, my father and I walked through snow to cut our Christmas tree, which we found among hundreds of evergreens growing on our ten-acre lot. Back inside, as they had for every Christmas I can remember, my father hung strings of multicolored tree lights while Mother brought out the ornaments. In the past my brother and I hung the ornaments together. This year he was not there. I felt his absence. Afterward, we placed packages—several we had purchased for each other and one for each of us that my brother had sent—under the tree.

On Christmas Eve the three of us went to church where we heard more talk about the war. Parishioners inquired politely about college life and I assured them that my studies were going well. Everyone wanted to know where Harold, Jr. was and if he was safe.

"He's still stateside," my father replied.

"He's safe so far," Mother added.

On Christmas day my brother called from Fort Meade, Maryland. We thanked him for his presents and asked if he had received orders. No news. After Christmas dinner Mother washed dishes while my father and I listened to the radio in the living room.

"You know Woods have always been Army," he said again. "You and Harold are continuing that tradition. I'm extremely proud."

He was uncharacteristically serious. No jokes.

"It doesn't look good for the country right now, but we'll get it turned around," he added.

I respected my father and felt gratified to have earned his pride.

"We're fighting two wars this time," I said, showing off what I had learned at school.

"Yes, with two oceans protecting us, but so many are dead already," he said with a sigh. "You know son, sometimes a necessary evil is right to triumph over wrong. It's patriotism. God will understand and forgive. You'll endure physical hardships—the training, the lack of food, and plenty of confusion—but you will have to trust and obey your superiors. The Army looks after its own. Just do your duty. I just pray that the war will end soon."

When I returned to school, newspapers and radio broadcasts continued to feature news about war. I read or heard reports about Japanese-Americans forced into relocation camps, bombs falling on London and Okinawa, and casualties in the Philippines. Douglas MacArthur's army surrendered, and US troops were taken captive. Our Navy lost battles in the Pacific. Even Australia was threatened for a while. Singapore fell. In my classes, new professors explained how former professors had taken government jobs or had been called to active duty. Classmates began to disappear.

I finished my school year, returned home to my summer job of sweeping floors and waiting on customers at Coon's store. With the construction of their retirement home complete, Mother's routine of washing, ironing, playing bridge, shopping for groceries, cleaning house, and cooking had returned to normal. Dad cultivated and planted a large vegetable garden, cut down dead trees, and mowed grass. He walked to the Bomoseen post office to pick up our mail and talk with friends. At dinner he talked about what other men in town were doing to help in the war effort. During the evening, he listened to the news and read the *Rutland Herald*. He studied want ads for job vacancies created by the draft. He'd say this company or that company had openings, or he'd talk about rationing.

When I returned to Philadelphia to begin my second year, military police guarded dormitories and entrances to the quadrangle. Extracurricular activities stopped. Fewer men were left on campus. At the nearby Horn and Hardart automat, a woman sat in the middle of the room with a sugar bowl, allowing only a half teaspoon of sugar for each cup of coffee and no sugar at all on grapefruit or anything else. White Castle hamburgers (my favorite lunch) had disappeared. I couldn't even buy a pair of shoes without first going to a rationing board.

Soon after classes resumed, Mother wrote that my father had taken a job in Springfield, Vermont, forty miles from Bomoseen, at the Fellows Gear Shaper Company that produced machines used to manufacture airplanes and tanks. He had taken a room there, and commuted home on the weekends. Mother moved to the Fair Haven Inn.

Again, we heard from my brother but this time through VMail from the China–Burma–India Theater, where he was helping to build the Lido Road. He hadn't been in ground fighting but had experienced air raids. I could see the unspoken worry on my parents' faces, wishing for my brother to be home again, safe. I worried, too.

A month later, back at school, I was preparing for final exams when I received a Western Union Telegram dated February 1, 1943: "Army wire received. Close up accounts and come home. Love, Dad." Like so many others, I obtained a leave of absence from the university and returned home.

Induction

On Saturday, February 20, 1943, my parents drove me to the bus station in Fair Haven. This time, as we waved goodbyes to each other, tears welled up in my eyes and began to stream down my face. I wondered if I would ever see them again. As the bus turned the corner, my parents, still waving, disappeared in a blur. I said silent prayers asking God to comfort my parents and protect my brother and me.

I walked around Philadelphia, ending up at Wanamaker's, where I bought a green, leatherbound 1943 diary small enough to fit into my shirt pocket, a sewing kit, a khaki-covered Webster's dictionary, and a shaving kit. The sewing kit was a suggestion from Mother. I bought the diary to record my experiences of Army life; my Father had kept one during his tour of France in the First World War. The dictionary, I felt, would keep me connected somehow to my academic studies, a way of taking college with me. I slept in my old dorm room.

On Sunday, after church, while eating lunch at the Horn and Hardart, I met four classmates. Our bond in that moment was the common knowledge that each of us had entered military life. We left the restaurant together and walked around campus, stopping before a statue of Benjamin Franklin for photographs. We vowed to reunite at that statue in four years, if we were still alive.

Afterwards, back in my room, I made my first entry in my war diary: the names of students with whom I vowed a reunion: Ted, Jess, Jim, and Charley. I never heard from or saw them again.

The following morning, dressed in gray wool slacks, a brown and black plaid sports jacket, and a white shirt, I carried a small bag filled with my purchases from Wanamaker's and a khaki-covered New Testament with psalms Rev. Wells had given me, and joined a hundred young men at the dorm entrance. An officer read our names in alphabetical order, instructing us to queue up in one of four lines.

An Army band played "Over There" as we sought the cadence and tried to step in time with the music. We marched six blocks. Philadelphia locals lining the route waved and cheered us on (waving back was prohibited). Little boys ran alongside us, as if they, too, were going to war. Periodically, girls appeared from the waving crowd to stand closer to our marching line. Having caught sight of a familiar face, they plunged themselves into our rhythm to hug and kiss one of the men. American flags swirled back and forth in the crowd. Handheld signs read: "Good Luck," "See You Soon," and "Give 'Em Hell."

Army buses met us at the station for transport to Fort Meade, Maryland, where an officer lined us up to march to the dispensary and another officer commanded us to strip to our shorts and shoes.

Individually, we walked from room to room to be interviewed and inspected. In Room A, an Army doctor checked my lungs, heart and blood pressure, and noted his findings on a chart. He sent me, chart in hand, to room B. Rooms C and D followed.

In Room E, I met the psychiatrist. "Are you opposed to war?" he asked.

"No, sir."

"Married?"

"No, sir."

"Do you like girls?"

"Yes, sir."

I knew what he was trying to do. I played stupid. I didn't want to be singled out for any reason.

"I see you enlisted. Why did you enlist?"

"My family always enlists, sir."

"Next!"

In another room I left a urine sample.

A "short arm" greeted me in the next room: I had to peel back the foreskin of my penis, allowing a doctor's examination for venereal diseases. I feared getting an erection: I didn't, thank God.

In the final room, I received two shots.

After our physicals, we marched to a supply building, received uniforms, marched to the mess hall to eat, then marched to our temporary barracks, where talk flowed in all kinds of accents—from Brooklyn, Georgia, North Carolina, Maine, New Jersey, from all over the country.

"Hey, we got ourselves some college boys here."

"Where's the bathroom?"

"It's not a bathroom, it's a latrine, stupid. You're in the Army now."

"See that one over there. Looks like he's shy about undressing with all of us standin' around. How about we go over and watch?"

"If you snore, buddy, I'm going to kick your bed so hard you'll go flying to the other side of the room."

I prayed to be invisible.

The following morning, in the February cold, I boarded a troop train and slept in a Pullman car that carried me to Camp Wolters in Mineral Wells, Texas, where I spent thirteen weeks in basic training.

Rectangular, with a white clapboard exterior and a gray shingled roof, my barracks looked exactly like one hundred or more other barracks in neat rows on both sides of the street. Inside the barracks were rows of beds covered by brown Army blankets tucked in, squared corners, over white sheets and a pillow. At the foot of my bed sat my footlocker with "Robert W. Wood" stenciled in white. I hung my uniform on a wooden rod surmounted by a wooden shelf where my caps and helmet were properly placed. My bed—an end bed—flanked a wooden partition, separating the sleeping area from the latrine.

At the sound of reveille each morning, training began. Carrying thirty-pound field packs and a rifle, we ran obstacle courses, learned to throw hand grenades and fire machine guns and mortars. We hiked for miles and wore gas masks through a gas chamber. We pitched our pup tents, took them down, moved, and pitched them again. At the rifle range, we learned to judge distances and improve our aim. I was not the fastest or most accurate, but I improved over time.

After training, the latrine became a busy place filled with steam and twenty or more nude male bodies with skimpy bath towels wrapped around them, walking to and from a communal shower. Surprisingly, I was too tired to think sexual thoughts.

During the evenings I stayed in the barracks, watching poker and crap games and listening to bull sessions. I joined in discussions about the war and government policy and avoided conversations about gambling, girls, or how to swipe food from the mess hall. After our commander shouted, "lights out," my tired body welcomed the bed. Sleep came quickly, and I didn't hear a sound until the next morning when the routine started over again.

In addition to the physical training, we studied manuals and books of regulations, attended lectures, and saw training films. We learned to salute and say, "yes, sir" and "no, sir." We memorized our serial numbers, the different insignias for rank and how to obey orders; we learned the difference between combat ribbons and a good conduct ribbon, and the grounds for a dishonorable discharge—desertion, cowardice under fire, disobeying orders, murder, mutiny, and being "suspected" of being a homosexual.

Such rules weighed on me, but I had grown accustomed to concealing my sexual feelings. It might have been saltpeter in our food or the fatigue of training or the strict time schedule, but after a month of basic training everyone began to look the same, physically, even in a latrine full of nude men. We were all looking better, fitter. We all bragged about the number of push-ups and rifle lifts we could do.

We looked out for one another: we made unmade beds and cleaned unclean rifles; we even lied for our buddies, because we wanted our barrack to be judged the best. Several of my barrack friends sought my assistance with words and spelling when they wrote letters. Perhaps the most important way we supported one another was to tolerate what we didn't like about each other.

Men cursed, even using the Lord's name in vain, and I didn't like it: perhaps because I had been raised a Christian and assigned a moral judgment to the words. Yet, when a fellow soldier, having received a letter from home informing him that his older brother had been killed in action, began to rant, "Those yellow sons of bitches. I'll kill the bastards," I sympathized with his emotions.

More difficult for me was the banter that I heard, although it was seldom directed at me:

"Did you hear the story about two queers who got into a fight and threw powder puffs at each other? One sprained his wrist." Laughter.

"Ok, which son-of-a-bitch shortsheeted my bunk? If I catch him, I'll carve my initials on his ass."

"Lights out men."

"Now dream about your favorite broad."

"I'm going to dream about the captain's wife."

"I don't want any of you fairies dreaming about me."

"Hey, did you hear they picked up a guy last night for giving somebody a blow job?"

Seven weeks into training I was assigned a message to deliver across camp. I walked alone through a section of camp where I hadn't been before and passed an open fenced-in area approximately fifty feet square. Guards posted at each corner atop four, ten-foot high observation towers kept watch. Barbed wire surrounded the area.

Without slowing down, I glanced through barbed wire. Men stood in the open area, whites and blacks together. I looked again and noticed "Q" written on the backs of three of the men. "Queer" flashed in my mind like a neon light over a roadside diner flashing "EAT." It was like an electric shock: men like me had been caught.

After I delivered the message, I retraced my steps outside the stockade, trying not to appear concerned. All I could see was "Q." None of the other men were wearing a brand. That night, by flashlight, lying in my bunk, feeling confused and threatened, I wrote the letter "Q" in my war diary, in pencil in case I had to erase it.

My mates hung pin-up girls or pictures of girlfriends and talked freely about sexual conquests, dates, and perfumed letters from home, all of which I could see were great morale boosters. But I couldn't even be suspected of having the sexual feelings that came naturally to me. The "Q" in my diary came to stand for my unspoken resentment and anger at a double standard.

Six weeks later, my last day of training, was my biggest day since high school graduation. We were given one weekend to celebrate and say our goodbyes to friends. We talked about potential orders separating us to various parts of the world: it was generally believed that shipment to the West Coast meant you would be shipped to Asia, while shipment to the East meant Europe. Orders were kept secret.

On Monday, I boarded a troop train to Camp Shenango, Pennsylvania, where training continued less rigorously. We had time to catch up on news. The Allies invaded Sicily, marking the first use of paratroopers. Italians had revolted against Mussolini. Our side seemed to be winning. I thought, hoped, maybe this thing will be over before I'll have to fight.

Eventually, I boarded trains to Camp Patrick Henry near Newport News, Virginia, and Camp Shanks, New York. On an eight-hour pass, a group of us caught a bus for Manhattan.

Gaping at skyscrapers and electric signs, I walked along Broadway to Times Square and the Pepsi-Cola Canteen, which was supplied with writing desks, paper and envelopes, pay telephones, hot showers, trays of donuts, and all the Pepsi Cola you could drink. I called home.

My father answered,

"Where are you, son?"

"I'm on liberty in the middle of Times Square."

"Times Square? Watch out for pickpockets. Any news yet?"

"I expect orders any day now. Any news from Harold?"

"Yes, he's still building roads. He's safe. Let me let you speak to your mother. Take care of yourself. You're in our prayers. We're proud of you, son."

"Bobby, is that you? Are you alright?" Mother asked.

"I'm fine. Still no word. Don't worry Mother. I'm going to be okay."

"I've got the whole church praying for you," she said before she started to cry.

"I'll be home before you know it. Try not to worry. I'm headed to a dance hall with some of my buddies. I'll let you know as soon as I know."

"That sounds nice. I'm sure you'll find a pretty girl to dance with."

"Yes. Look, I've got to hang up. People are waiting to use the phone."

"Don't forget we love you." Now I was holding back tears.

The dance hall in Times Square had a huge dance floor spotted by dots from a rotating mirrored ball. A live band played jitterbug and big band tunes. Pretty girls stood around the room. Light spots covered the couples dancing on the floor. I watched my buddies scan the room for dance partners. Before long they were dancing.

"Aren't you going to dance?" one of them asked.

"No, I think I'll sit this one out."

I watched them dance with one girl after another. They seemed to enjoy the physical closeness of a girl, as if these were the last days they would touch a tender hand or feel whatever passion raced through their veins. I envied them.

I left the dance hall after a while, walked around Times Square and bought some postcards. A prostitute followed me saying, "this way soldier."

"No, thanks," I said.

I went inside a movie theater to see *Holiday Inn*. When Bing Crosby sang "White Christmas," I felt homesick.

Another prostitute tapped me on the shoulder. "Looking for some action?" she whispered.

"No, leave me alone," I said.

Afterwards, I ran to the bus station and caught the last bus back to the base. Some of the men bragged about sexual conquests in a vulgar way. Like me, most of the men rode back to the base in silence.

Unit Cohesion

On August 24, 1943, along with three hundred Army soldiers, a Navy crew, and enough Marines to man anti-aircraft guns, I sailed aboard a Liberty Ship from Newport News, Virginia, bound for an unknown destination across the Atlantic. While the Navy crew went about their sailing duties, Marines remained stationed at their guns. GI's lounged on deck during the day and as often as we could at night. We were told that the deck was the safest place to be if our ship should be hit by a torpedo or run into a mine.

Ocean storms tossed the ship and tested our stomachs. After sunset, lights on deck were forbidden but we remained there until ordered below. I counted stars and tried to make out the silhouettes of nearby ships.

One night warning whistles sounded, and we heard explosions, and saw a nearby ship in flames, probably hit by a German submarine. I looked out over the dark ocean and saw shapes of the exploded vessel and men floating. Down below, as I lay in my bunk, I wept, sad for the destroyed ship and dead men. Lying flat on my stomach using a flashlight, I read the Bible, hoping to calm my fear.

"Dear God, keep us safe," I prayed. "Keep this ship and my buddies safe, and bring us to land, soon. In Jesus' name. Amen."

Unable to sleep, I listened to the bunk-to-bunk banter.

"We're headed for England, I'll bet."

"Why teach us French if we were going to England?"

"Wanna bet?"

After eighteen days at sea, we saw shore lights, a French Vichy flag, then an American flag. Rumors spread but we still didn't know for sure until we unloaded at Camp Don B. Passage in Casablanca, North Africa. There, I saw Moorish domed buildings scattered across the landscape. Veiled women walked among camels, soldiers in French and British uniforms, and military vehicles.

Soon after, enclosed in a letter from Mother, was the following prayer:

> God, Father of Freedom, look after that boy of mine, wherever he may be. Walk in upon him. Talk with him during the silent watches of the night and spur him to bravery when he faces the cruel foe. Transfer my prayer to his heart.
>
> Keep my boy inspired by the never-dying faith in his God. Throughout all the long days of a hopeful victory, wherever his duty takes him, keep his spirit high, and his purpose unwavering. Make him a loyal friend. Nourish him with the love that I gave to him at birth and satisfy the hunger of his soul with the knowledge of my daily prayer.

> He is my constant treasure. Take care of him, God. Keep him in health and sustain him under every possible circumstance. I once warmed him under my heart. You warm him anew in his shelter under the stars. Touch him with my smile of cheer and comfort, and my full confidence in his every brave pursuit.
>
> Fail him not and may he not fail You, his country, nor the mother who bore him."

Her prayer felt like a blanket of protection, and I kept it close to me.

Soon, most of us were in forty-and-eight (forty men or eight horses) boxcars, rolling over hot, dry, desert terrain. A sliding door on each side of the car remained open, allowing hot, dry air to pass through. I sat on my barracks bag against one of the walls, close enough to the side doors that I could see out.

Along the way I saw trees split horizontally, broken two or three feet above the ground, and charred military vehicles. Bandaged soldiers and civilians, some on crutches, walked through rubble. We rolled an entire week, through Fez and Oran to Bizerte. Near the port in Bizerte, I saw ships sunk in the harbor and buildings destroyed by bombs or filled with bullet holes. Anxiety grew within me to match the open-mouthed shock I often felt from the sights.

When the train stopped in Bizerte, I, along with two hundred other men, received assignments to join a sixty-millimeter mortar replacement pool. We were strangers, bodies waiting for orders.

I became one of two supply men in a five-man mortar squad. Like my counterpart, I carried a canvas vest with six shells, each resembling a foot-long torpedo with three fins on the end. Six shells added about ten pounds of weight to my pack and rifle. When my shells were used up, I ran half a mile to an ammunition depot, refilled my vest and returned, shells bouncing on my chest and back. I had to get back before the other supply man's six shells were used up. We depended upon each other to function. We were a team.

Mortar practice began just after breakfast and continued until supper. Sight, load, fire, move, explosion, load, fire, move, explosion, load, fire, move, explosion, all day long running back and forth to the depot. We practiced with real ammunition now.

This is combat, I thought. I am here amid it. My twelfth birthday came to mind, God's gift of ninety more years. I used that memory and prayers to coach myself not to be afraid. I prayed mostly for strength and courage to measure up in the heat of battle.

On October 1, 1943, along with three hundred other soldiers, I boarded a military ship. Trucks, tanks, jeeps, and other military vehicles were stored below. There were no bunks on board, so many soldiers slept downstairs in the vehicles. I slept on deck as I had when we had crossed the ocean.

Rumors started and spread throughout the ship. We heard about the horrible fighting in the battle for Naples. Maybe we're headed there, many thought. Our minds rehearsed the moment when the front of the boat would let down and we would go ashore. After four days we could see Sicily and Salerno, where three weeks earlier the Allies had staged a hard-fought beach landing.

When the front of the ship let down, my comrades and I walked into ankle-high water and waded with our rifles and barracks bags to Paestum Beach. Three thoughts flashed in and out of my mind: Keep your rifle dry, follow the fellows in front of you, and nobody is shooting from behind the shattered trees and buildings on the beach.

Somehow, we made it to shore. The Temple of Neptune, built around 450 BCE, was being used as an AID station. Others paid for our safe landing with their lives.

We boarded Army transport trucks that sped down a paved road, passed more damaged buildings and twisted trees with their tops blown off. Burned, exploded trucks had been abandoned. Farm animals wandered on the side of the road. Telephone lines dangled and wrecked military vehicles littered the landscape.

We rode along the sea, two or three miles north of Naples, until we reached an apple orchard—rows of apple and olive trees with low branches six feet off the ground, a perfect cover. Small red apples and green olives covered the ground. Farmers sold us walnuts by the helmet-full, and there were plenty of cider apples to eat with our "C" rations.

In that orchard I joined my permanent outfit: Company I, 3rd Battalion, 142nd Infantry Regiment, and the 36th Division, comprised mostly men from the Texas and Oklahoma National Guard. I was in the weapons platoon. Men from the 36th had been together for years; they suffered forty percent casualties.

A sergeant paired us up to pitch tents: I worked with another mortar man from the 36th. As we worked, he explained the meaning behind our division insignia:

"The Arrowhead stands for Oklahoma and the T for Texas," he said before describing the chain of command, and recalling the invasion at Salerno. "The Italians had surrendered, so we weren't expectin' them to open up on us. But the Germans hadn't surrendered and were waitin' for us up in the hills. And they opened fire on us, and we were droppin' all over the place."

He didn't mention names, but I felt I had replaced a close friend.

The Texan and I cleared a space for our tent under an apple tree, making a small mound of apples, which we were allowed to eat, on one side. We took off our packs and pulled out our shelter halves—pup tents with large buttons on one side and buttonholes on the other. We buttoned them together as if we had been buttoning for months. Then we pulled out collapsible tent posts, each about a yard high. Each had a spike at the top, which went through an eyelet in the tent. I sat on the ground, holding the two posts, while my new buddy stretched and staked the buttoned canvases over me. Then, using a pick and shovel, we dug a ditch around the edge of the tent to drain off any water and a foxhole.

My buddy took his shirt off outside, sat down, and backed in; then he took off his shoes and pants and crawled under our blankets. He yelled, "All clear." As I was taking off my shirt, I looked up and saw a stone farmhouse I had seen earlier that day.

The farmhouse had a thatched roof and a chimney on one end, with curls of smoke wafting out of it into the air. I could smell the wood smoke. I noticed a well in the front yard (an endless supply of fresh water) and laundry still hanging out front to dry. As I looked through opened shutters and a large window, I saw the faces of a family lit by the glow of candle-light. Seeing them around their dinner table reminded me of home: I missed home.

Inside the tent the Texan and I shared just thirty square feet to store our equipment and sleep. We placed our helmets upside down in the back of the tent, where it came to a point. I used my helmet to store my wristwatch, diary, and Bible. I made a pillow out of my shirt, jacket and pants, and placed my shoes, canteen, flashlight, and rifle next to the outside edge of the tent.

I smelled ripe apples and listened to a chorus of snores, the footsteps of guards on duty, a dog barking, and the sound of chickens and roosters at the farmhouse. I slept.

The following day, barefoot farm girls with purple, wine-stained legs, wearing well-worn dresses, came to watch us exercise and drill. They had been stomping grapes.

I was sitting beside my tent, writing a letter home, when one of the girls came by.

"Vino?" she asked. I tried some but didn't care for it.

One of my GI neighbors noticed her.

"You want to come into my tent?" he asked. He waved Italian money in the air. She walked over to him.

"Vino?" she asked.

He took the wine. She took the money, then crawled into his tent. I heard giggles, grunts, and sighs. I could see her feet entwined in Army boots sticking out from the tent, and thought, you'd better hurry before you get caught fraternizing with the locals. I didn't bemoan that soldier a moment of pleasure. Who didn't yearn for closeness with another human being when their life hung in the balance?

Later, in the middle of calisthenics and without warning, sirens sounded, and orders came for us to hide under trees, out of sight. Enemy reconnaissance planes flew low. Our company commander ordered gunners to hold their fire so as not to reveal our position. The planes didn't return.

It began to rain, and we continued to train, eat, and sleep. As I tried to write letters home, I heard explosions of big guns in the distance and felt the ground shake. At times, I felt fear, which intensified when the command came from our platoon leader: "Strike your tents, we are moving out in two hours."

We disassembled our tents, packed our backpacks, filled our canteens, and posted letters. Farm girls and soldiers said their goodbyes. Some of the girls cried, waving scarves as we marched down a dirt road to load up in Army trucks. Wearing raincoats, we sat in open trucks on wooden benches, eight on each side, with our rifles between our legs. One girl ran up to the truck. "I fuck. I fuck," she shouted and waved her scarf. The men laughed. Why did they have to teach her that word?

In the dim light of dusk our convoy of twenty trucks with black tape over the headlights and taillights started down a muddy road. The soldiers they carried bounced against each other. I pressed my feet into the floor and leaned back to hold myself in place. When it rained, I hunched over, holding my rifle under the seat to keep it dry. Water dripped down my collar. We rode for three hours then stopped without warning.

"Get out, double time," officers commanded in whispers.

Members of my mortar squad located each other and joined our weapons platoon—a machine gun squad, a squad of riflemen, and a medic.

Marching along the side of the road, we fell in line with other platoons. In the shadows I saw more shattered trees and blown-up buildings. Like a wet blanket around my head, I smelled gunpowder, sulfurous and heavy. Then, at a sergeant's command, platoons began splitting off.

That night my platoon looked for dry spots under trees, where it was damp but not muddy. We paired up and pitched tents in the rain. I had a new buddy.

We didn't know who or what lurked behind the shadows. Lights were forbidden, silence ordered. We heard cannonading, louder now, and trucks moving in the darkness.

Sheer exhaustion allowed me to sleep that night. The next day we walked through farm fields toward a river. Commanders instructed, "We're headed for the other side of the river. Rafts are waiting. Enter them quickly and quietly. Use the paddles. Try to keep your squad together."

We were marching through a cabbage field, still wet from rain, with a sour cabbage smell. I heard the river, swollen from the rain, then gunfire. Bullets began to hit the ground all around us. Dirt erupted; cabbages split. Troops scattered. Confused, I fell to my stomach and crawled on my elbows.

"I'm hit, medic, medic," a soldier to my left screamed.

I wanted to stop and help but recalled the lesson from training to "leave the wounded for the medics." I kept crawling, trying to hide behind cabbages. I panicked. Almost hyperventilating, I thought, why weren't we warned? Why didn't someone tell us? Where was our artillery? I couldn't see anyone to shoot. Where were they?

"Keep moving, work your way to the river," an officer shouted. Finally, big guns behind us fired, and our artillery shells swooshed overhead. I stopped crawling. I heard explosions on the other side of the river. The ground shook. I shook. Oh, my God! Seven incredibly loud explosions jolted the cabbage field and our bodies before the guns went silent and the officer shouted again, "Keep moving. We're almost there."

I continued to crawl to the edge of the river. No shots came. We crawled randomly, three or four at a time, into black rubber rafts, and paddled across the river, wondering when more shots would come.

On the other side, searching again for my squad, I saw a man in German uniform lying motionless. I crouched, facing the man, pointing my rifle at his chest. I was ready to kill him: I wouldn't have given it a second thought.

"Save your ammo, Wood. He's dead."

I looked again at his dead body and felt something like pity for him.

After the river, we climbed up, up, up in steep mountainous terrain on the way to Monte Casino, a historic abbey on top of a mountain, which served as an observation point for the Germans. The abbey had a view of the entire Liri Valley all the way to Naples.

When not engaged in actual combat, I hauled supplies—ammunition, food, water, and mail—up and down the mountain. Constant rain and miles of telephone wires going to the front lines made the steep, narrow mountain paths treacherous under foot. The ammunition depot was much further away than it had been in practice, and relocating my mortar team was much more difficult. Constant climbing caused my legs to ache. Blisters swelled on my feet from wet shoes. My clothes were either damp or soaked. My body itched. Keep up, I thought. Keep up.

Germans positioned on top of the mountain had an advantage. We moved into positions previously held by our enemy who knew the terrain and the location of caves, the only natural shelters there.

Both sides fought, using probing actions—troops would scout the territory and report back. We never knew for sure if the enemy was ten feet or miles away. As we moved up the mountain, fighting became regular, day after day of gunfire and shells coming over our heads and nothing really being resolved. Rain continued to pour. The higher we climbed, the colder it became. My tent was soaked.

I didn't understand the purpose of all this. I felt constant alarm and fear, and the stench of constant acrid smells—the smell of death.

One night I sat on a stone before crawling into my pup tent to sleep. I looked at the stars and relished a moment of peace, then across our encampment to see the rest of my platoon. Those who smoked covered their lights, and those who talked, whispered. The rain had stopped momentarily. Smells of dampness hung heavy. I was eating a biscuit C Ration when unfamiliar sounds, rustling sounds, like someone brushing against tree branches, came from below. The sounds grew louder, and the men smoking snuffed their cigarettes. Everyone grew quiet. We instinctively picked up our rifles and moved for cover.

I crouched behind a rock, listening. Alarm infused my senses as I heard rifle fire, then bullets whizzing around us, landing in the dirt and trees, and ricocheting off rocks. Some of our men screamed and moaned from wounds. Confusion replaced alarm, as if we were in an animal stampede.

"The bastards are down in front of us, let 'em have it," one of our commanders shouted.

We shot into darkness, then launched several grenades. Explosions followed, then silence.

"Jones and Smith, make sure they're all dead," commanded a sergeant.

I crawled toward one of our wounded soldiers. Medics worked, ripping open his trousers, while I gave him water from my canteen. I found his rifle and brought it to him. Blood gushed from his left knee.

"How bad does it hurt?" the medic asked.

He poured sulfa powder into the wound.

"Can you stand the pain?"

"I'm fine. It takes more than one bullet to hurt me," he said.

Guards were posted. Still shaking, scared, and worried about when the next attack might come, I crawled over to a tree and leaned up against the cold, rough bark, my rifle in my lap. Fatigue wrestled with my fear. I entertained no thoughts about God or prayers. I just nodded off to sleep.

I was leaning on that tree the next morning when an officer woke me and asked how I was doing. I stood up but didn't salute him. Salutes in combat were forbidden because they telegraphed who were the officers.

"I'm okay."

"Remember to keep your head down when the fighting starts up again, and keep this down too," he said patting me on my butt.

With that simple gesture, I felt like Bob Wood just for a moment, almost human. I could have hugged him.

Mass confusion and uncertainty came with attacks. Soldiers didn't know for sure who or what to shoot at sometimes. Wounded soldiers screamed while officers shouted commands. I slipped and slid in mud and hid behind trees, all my senses assaulted at once—the sights of bloated, dismembered corpses; the sounds of guns, bombs, airplanes; the taste of dirt, mud, metal, and blood; the irritations of scrapes, pinches, bruises, blisters, stomach aches, and diarrhea. God had abandoned us, I thought.

Again, training kicked in.

"Keep up with your unit," they said in basic training. "If you get cut off and you don't know where the commanding officers are, or which direction you are supposed to go, you could get lost on the battlefield or end up being shot by one of your own."

Soldiers depended upon each other to carry an equal share of the load, to do what we had been trained to do, our personalities and sexual preferences notwithstanding. Bottom line: we would fight to defend each other's lives.

Combat created unit cohesion: we were in it together, especially when we heard "they're running, they're running, we've got the bastards running." Such words evoked incredible exhilaration.

I continued to write in my War Diary:

> 12–5–43. 11:30. Ache all over. Retreated last night, then returned. Tripped over dead feet. Everyone sick and grumpy. What next? Lost my overcoat.
>
> 12–7–43. Feet swollen. On guard, eleven to one, ten to twelve. Heavy shelling. Got some mail but no time to read it as busy fighting.
>
> 12–8–43. Read mail. Saw wild holly growing, and dandelions still in bloom. Hope division gets relieved soon.
>
> 12–10–43. Sleeping with Pete. Have five blankets for the two of us. Shoes off. Toes still sore. Clothes caked with mud. Full moon. Some snow.
>
> 12–13–43. Morale down. Learned we are going forward instead of being relieved. Everyone badly in need of leggings. Goodness knows what will happen tonight. God be with me.

I caught a glimpse of a creator God in the wild holly, blooming dandelions, and in a full moon that cast a glow over the battlefield. Amid the destruction, I could see beauty. I prayed, thanking God food, asking for safety. Once or twice, I wondered if God approved of all the destruction and suffering. In those moments, I doubted God's providence. Such doubts intensified a sense of doom.

Carried Down a Mountain

Close to the front lines, our platoon camped in a small cave littered with empty German food supply boxes and cigarette packages. We used latrines and foxholes the Germans left behind; at least we didn't have to dig.

Bruno from Chicago and I were assigned guard duty on our first night there. Darkness came and we checked our machine gun mounted in front of the foxhole to make sure that it was loaded with an ammunition belt before we jumped into the hole. We watched and listened while the rest of our platoon slept in the cave ten feet behind us. Silence surrounded us.

We leaned against the back of the foxhole, stamping our feet to keep them warm, and nudged each other from time to time to keep ourselves from falling asleep. After several hours I heard footsteps on the wet ground and branches breaking.

"Halt! Angus?" I called.

I waited to hear the password of "beef."

No answer came.

As I opened my mouth to shout "Angus" again, I heard a rifle fire and felt a pressure—like being hit with a fast baseball—in the center of my chest, knocking the air out of me. My legs went rubbery. Before blacking out, I managed to grab the handle of the machine gun, and squeeze, causing the gun to sound off and spit out bullets. By that time Bruno crumpled to the bottom of the foxhole.

I regained consciousness in a cave, stretched out on a litter, wrapped in bloody bandages, a medic's tag dangling from my side.

The next day four buddies carried me down the mountain. Since I was in and out of consciousness, I cannot remember much about the men, not even their names. I remember the men struggling to keep the stretcher level while they negotiated the steep mountain terrain, and airplanes flying overhead. At the bottom of the mountain, they hailed an Army Jeep, and placed me, still strapped in my stretcher, across the hood. I owe my life to those men who carried me down that mountain.

A Calling

"This one's alive!" a nurse said, looking down at me lying on the dirt floor when I had become momentarily conscious.

Daylight streamed in from under the flaps of the tent. Above me doctors, nurses, and orderlies worked in a large field hospital, a MASH unit.

Throughout the night I woke from one deep sleep just to fall back into another. When awake, I heard moans and groans on either side of me and struggled to see the source of such sounds of misery. In the darkness I saw bodies on stretchers covered with Army blankets, wounded soldiers, an injured body gridlock. No one seemed to be tending to us. I felt weak, near-death weak. There were times when I couldn't feel my arms and feet. God don't let me be paralyzed, I prayed. Once during the night, I touched the bandage on my chest, feeling for blood: there was none. I wondered if I was bleeding internally. Surprisingly, I felt little pain. I woke up on the ground, barely able to move my head.

"Yes, I'm alive," I thought. An eerie silence replaced moans and groans around me, as bodies beside me remained motionless, without breath. I could barely move.

Explosions shook the earth, causing the canvas tentflaps to flutter. I shut my eyes, so weak I was oblivious to the commotion.

Moments later, smelling coffee and bacon and sensing people—doctors and nurses, perhaps—walking toward me, I produced enough voice to say, "when do I get some breakfast?"

I felt myself being lifted. Those lifting me placed me on an operating table and turned me gently, so I lay on my left side. My right arm fell limp in front of me. Someone asked me to raise it, but I couldn't. My blanket fell to the ground. Doctors and nurses worked behind me. I felt a needle stick in my right side.

"We have some infection in here," I heard someone say. A nurse held my hand.

She pulled a cardboard box from under the cot, and showed me my wristwatch, diary, and New Testament. Seeing that Bible caused me to think about Jesus. He is aware of my need, I thought. Feeling His grace flowing toward me comforted me, reassured me.

That same day a doctor explained how a bullet had entered and exited my body, leaving a hole about the size of a dime in the center of my chest and a slightly larger hole in my back just below my right shoulder.

"You're one lucky, soldier," he said. "It missed your vital organs."

By the grace of God, I thought.

"Infection is the problem," he told me. "You almost drowned in the infection."

In the weeks that followed, doctors repeatedly drained the infection. Since I was too weak to sit up, a hospital orderly sat by my cot and fed me meals of hot oatmeal, toast, coffee, milk, scrambled eggs, and cocoa. A nurse washed my face, arms, chest, and rubbed my back with alcohol and powder. Two stoves and plenty of blankets kept me warm. I was safe.

One day I heard Christmas carols and noticed pine boughs and holly hanging from the top of the tent, and I thought about Jesus being born in a manger. An orderly gave me an orange and some candy, saying, "Merry Christmas." I was listening to laughter, glasses clinking, and Christmas music playing on a Victrola, when the chaplain came by again.

He sat on the stool and held my hand. "How are you doing, soldier? You know it's Christmas. Would you like me to write another letter to your folks?"

When I finished dictating my letter, the Chaplain asked me about my denominational affiliation.

"Congregational," I told him.

"Would you like to have a Christmas prayer?"

"Sure."

"Oh Lord Jesus, as we pause to celebrate your birthday in this foreign country, we ask Thy healing presence in this field hospital and with this soldier," he prayed. "Touch him with the gift of healing. Comfort his parents and let health return to his body. Amen."

I hoped God would hear that chaplain's prayer, touch my weak body, and caress my parent's worried hearts. I hoped God would touch the grieving hearts of all who had received sad news—announcements of death, news of suffering. I was thinking more and more about death and suffering. I hoped God would restore peace in the world. So much was being hoped from God in those days.

I regained full consciousness in early January and became aware of a divine presence—no angels or anything like that, just the feeling everything would turn out well.

That same month I was transferred to a new, nine-story stone building with real beds, the 300th General Hospital in Naples. Another team of doctors examined me, and concerned about the ongoing infection, decided to operate.

"We think we found the source of your infection: a German must have stuck you with a dirty bayonet," the surgeon said after the surgery.

He pointed out a drainage tube that he inserted into the wound.

Bedridden, I faced a wall. Men in beds on either side of me faced the center aisle, and I was vaguely aware of another row of beds lining the other side of the room.

I had too much time to think. Combat was a constant assault on my emotions. Blood and dead bodies overwhelmed me at times, particularly the smell. I'll never forget those repulsive smells. I remembered the dead soldiers, and remembering them produced despair and guilt, which overwhelmed me so much that my prayers and beliefs seemed empty, without meaning. During these sad days, I was drawn to Psalm 91:

> You who live in the shelter of the Most High,
> who abide in the shadow of the Almighty,
> will say to the Lord, "My refuge and my fortress;
> my God, in whom I trust."
> For he will deliver you from the snare of the hunter
> and from the deadly pestilence;
> he will cover you with his pinions,
> and under his wings you will find refuge;
> his faithfulness is a shield and defense.

You will not fear the terror of the night
  or the arrow that flies by day
or the pestilence that stalks in darkness
  or the destruction that wastes at noonday.
A thousand may fall at your side,
  ten thousand at your right hand,
  but it will not come near you.
You will only look with your eyes
  and see the punishment of the wicked.
Because you have made the Lord your refuge,
  the Most High your dwelling place,
no evil shall befall you,
  no scourge come near your tent.

For weeks I read and reread it. Meanings began to crystallize in my mind: There is a power greater than me, and this power cares about me. This power is loyal and will protect me in my darkness—in the sadness and guilt I was feeling. Many have died and are dying, but I have been spared. Why? There must be a purpose.

Months passed. Soldiers around me cursed a lot. Some blamed God for their predicament; others blamed the Virgin Mary; most blamed Hitler or the Germans. I didn't have much anger or resentment for some reason. I continued to offer prayers for healing and felt grateful for cards and letters I received from church members in Fair Haven and Lorain.

After fifty-three days I stood on my own two feet and, like an infant, took a few steps, the first time I'd been on my feet since being wounded.

I spent three months in Naples and another month in Oran, North Africa, before I was carried on to the hospital ship, Acadia. The ship, without convoy, with lights aglow, made the ocean trip from Oran to Charleston, South Carolina, four days on the Mediterranean and eight days on the Atlantic.

During the voyage, I slept in a low bunk so my drainage tube could reach the glass jar on the floor. With me in that ward were forty-six leg amputees and three others recovering from chest wounds. I carried my glass jar everywhere I went—to the bathroom or to the sun deck just off our ward, where I spent most days reclined in a deck chair.

After a week in Charleston, I boarded a hospital train to Memphis, Tennessee, and the Kennedy General Hospital, which specialized in chest wounds. On my twenty-first birthday, a doctor removed my drainage tube.

The following week, having taken an overnight train from Vermont to Memphis, my mother and father quietly entered my room. Mother wore a hat and print dress, and Father wore a suit. Anxious, as if expecting a horrible sight, they looked me over. Mother began to cry. Father comforted her. Through her tears, Mother said, "thank you, God."

"Our prayers have been answered," Father said, while his eyes scanned me from head to toe.

Seeing the bandages around my chest, a shocked look came over him and he began to back away.

"You sure look good, Bob," he said.

They visited me each day. After three days they returned home.

In Memphis, I took anti-infection medication, met with doctors, read my Bible and letters from home, shopped at the PX, took in movies, shot pool, or played cards. On Sundays I attended chapel services and wrote to my parents. Before long I was strong enough to go home.

That Sunday, I wore my dress greens. Bandages still covered my wounds. I didn't preach exactly. Instead, I described my war experience. Dad mentioned that people at church wanted to hear how I had been wounded, so I told them. I talked also of my stays in hospitals, and the guilt I felt for surviving when so many had died. I told them about Psalm 91 and thanked them for their cards, letters, and prayers. I pleaded with them not to forget those still recovering in hospitals.

"There wasn't a dry eye in the congregation," my mother said afterwards.

A Physical Closeness

In November 1944, I walked through a portico built over a circular driveway that led to the central lobby of the Lake Placid Redistribution Center. The lobby was elegant, with plush carpets, hand-carved walnut walls, polished brass, wingback chairs, smoking stands, and a grand staircase. A ritzy place, I thought.

"Where do I report?" I asked a soldier, standing behind a reception desk.

"The Agora Section. I'll show you to your room," the soldier said after consulting his list.

He led me to a carpeted room furnished with two dressers, a wooden writing desk, two comfortable lounge chairs, and twin beds separated by a reading table. Two draped windows overlooked tennis courts. An attached tiled bathroom shined.

As I unpacked, my roommate, a short Irish corporal, greeted me.

"Let me introduce you to the former Lake Placid Club," he said, pulling out a map from an information packet on my desk.

"This is where we are," he said, pointing to our room on the map that he referenced while continuing, "and here is the theater, cross-country and downhill ski trails, the ice-skating rink, the toboggan runs and the mess hall, where, believe it or not, the food is delicious."

We exchanged stories about our outfits and injuries.

"I've been here two weeks shy of three months," the corporal said. "Take my word for it: you're going to like it here. No one works hard and you can get passes every weekend. We even have maids to make our beds and clean our rooms."

I was assigned to admitting patients, checking out those well enough to leave, and assigning rooms to those arriving.

Married couples occupied at least half the rooms in my section. As wives could only stay for three days, I saw many tearful reunions and goodbyes. While together, some of the couples seemed inseparable, stopping frequently to hug and kiss. I noticed the physical closeness between these men and women, as if they knew that life had given them another chance. Looking back, in contrast to the cold, bitter, horrible realities of combat, I think of those soldiers' reunions with their wives as a blessing. Although I had not experienced such a reunion, I could imagine how alive they must have felt through embraces, kisses, and the tactile pleasures of touching their lover's body. A stranger's letters were as close as I came to that experience.

At my father's request, Helen Turner, a girl from Youngstown, had written to say that she was praying for me and to ask questions about my health. What do the doctors say? Are you exercising? Are the bandages still on? How are you sleeping? Your last letter sounded like you may have a setback. You must be feeling much better. I felt her caring even though she was miles away. So touched was I by her concern, I sent her an orchid.

She sent a photograph of herself wearing the orchid. On the back of the picture she wrote, "your orchids and your girl." We hardly knew each other, yet her photograph gave me bragging rights.

When my roommate left Lake Placid to return to active duty, I did not assign another soldier to our room in his place. I had not slept alone since leaving my college dormitory. I welcomed the privacy. I remember thinking, I should be happy. I'm alive in these posh surroundings and feeling better each day, but I found myself crying alone in my room, so much so that I made an appointment with a therapist.

"Why do you think you're crying?" he asked.

"Because I'm lonely," I said. "I've been on the move for so long and I keep leaving people behind."

He remained silent for a while. "Any other reasons?"

"I don't know," I said. I knew but couldn't say.

Again, he waited.

"I just don't understand all the suffering," I said.

"You're not the only one who doesn't understand. You're only human. Just remember, it's good to cry. Don't keep those feelings bottled up. Let them out."

Although I felt as if I had been given permission to cry, I found myself recalling my father's advice to control my emotions. Through prayers I begged God to help me stop crying. Attending church helped me to think beyond myself and reminded me that I had a purpose for living, but still I cried. I made an appointment to see the chaplain, thinking he might be able to help.

"What can I do for you, soldier?" he asked. I scanned the ribbons on his uniform; he hadn't been in combat.

"Just needing to talk," I said. I talked about combat. He listened, without comment, or apparent concern or emotion as I tried to explain my desire to serve God.

"This happens a lot," he said. "I'll send your name to the Congregational Church headquarters, and they'll follow up if your interest in ministry remains once you return to college."

"Do you need any help conducting church services?" I asked.

"Army regulations don't permit it," he said. "But you might check with local pastors."

"I will," I said. We exchanged salutes, and I was about to walk out. "Just one more thing."

"Yes, soldier?"

"Why did God allow all this suffering?"

"My answer will not satisfy you," he said. "That question you will have to answer for yourself, and there are plenty of books that will help you find one."

I read *What Can I Believe? Why I Am a Christian?* and a history of Jesus, all checked out from the base library. Rev. Wells sent *The Will of the Lord* and *Elementary Psychology*. I took notes, which helped me prepare sermons for several churches in Lake Placid and back home in Fair Haven. I didn't find the answer to my questions on one page or in one book. I read, sometimes not understanding what I was reading. God, I came to believe, was familiar with suffering and love, having sent a Son to die for the world's salvation. And human beings, created in God's image, were free agents capable of evil. God loved human beings, including me, and Jesus showed the way of sacrificial love, which could transform people.

In March 1945, I wrote in my War Diary: "Revelation 21:5," which reads: "And the one who was seated on the throne said, 'See, I am making all things new.' Also he said, 'Write this, for these words are trustworthy and true.'" After Revelation 21:5, I wrote, "Is this me?"

Warm spring temperatures melted the snow and ice at Placid. A golf course and bicycle and hiking trails opened. I discovered great pleasure in taking walks in the woods. Alone among the rustic, natural scenes away from buildings and people, I enjoyed the budding trees and the sound of rippling creek water. Birds sang. In nature's sanctuary my mind replayed tapes of war, God and Jesus, and love. I saw couples walking together, hand in hand, and the sight would leave me feeling lonely. On my next furlough, I thought, I will visit Helen Turner.

When that time came, Helen waved at me from between her parents at Youngstown airport. She looked slim. Her long black hair swirled around her soft facial features. She wore a stylish coat and heels, and her smile made me feel welcome. She asked about my ribbons and medals on the way to their home in a residential section very similar to the one where I spent my childhood.

During dinner I answered her parents' questions about Army life and war and listened to Helen describe her work as a secretary in her father's law practice and outline the plans for the weekend. Through her demeanor and vocabulary, I sensed that she was educated. On Saturday Helen and I, accompanied by her mother, went to see a movie. We held hands. We all attended the Evergreen Presbyterian Church for Sunday worship, during which I was asked to speak. I thanked all those who sent cards and told them to pray for those still recovering. Later that afternoon Helen and I went to see another movie, again with her mother. Once again, we held hands. On Monday, with Helen's mother, we toured the Bancroft Elementary School, then went for a picnic in a park. On a blanket by a lake, I thanked Helen for all her letters.

"Did you write to other fellows?" I asked.

"No."

"I've heard that some girls write to five or six fellows."

"Not me," she said, and I felt honored.

I flew home the next day. My mother asked a lot of questions, but I had few answers.

Meanwhile, my brother Harold had written to announce his engagement to Jane Swift, a Fair Haven girl. They were to be married the following week in Pittsburgh, where Harold was stationed. Mother wrote that she and my father would not be attending Harold's wedding. Unable to attend myself, I sent them commemorative plates from the University of Pennsylvania. I was glad that my brother had fallen in love.

However, I still felt lonely.

One day a GI walked down the hallway past my desk, and I glanced up. He stared at me. I stared back. He smiled without looking away, and I looked up and down the corridor to see if anyone was in sight. We were alone. I put my hand out on the desk. He checked for hallway traffic. Seeing none, he put his hand on top of mine.

"Well finally!" he said. "My name is Scott."

I felt so excited that I couldn't speak for a moment.

"You came here three days ago."

"Yes," he said. "You assigned me my room."

He continued to gaze into my eyes.

"Yes, and you have a roommate?"

"Yes," he said. "Unfortunately."

"How about you?" he asked.

"No, but my room is in the middle of the hall. I wouldn't feel safe there," I said.

I looked up at the room board. By this time, fewer soldiers were arriving. The sixth, fifth, and fourth floors were already empty.

"401 is vacant," I said, knowing that 401 was a large, corner room with bay windows at the end of the hall.

"I will meet you there at 1700, when I get off duty. Everybody else will be in the mess hall."

"That sounds good to me," he said.

At 1700 I unlocked the door and followed Scott in, and quickly closed the door behind us, and locked it. Once inside, I scanned the room: the draperies were closed. Standing, we embraced each other. As I caressed his body with my hands, I felt his hands discovering me. He looked me in the eye, and asked, "Is the door locked?"

Scott tenderly kissed the scar on my chest. I closed my eyes, feeling that kiss, allowing it to be a salve of sorts. I found and gently kissed his scar, which began in the middle of his stomach. My lips followed his tender line, kissing along the way, until it came to his undershorts.

He groaned and rubbed his hand through my hair. I did the same. Feeling, seeing, and touching Scott was thrilling beyond words. We laughed in ecstasy. I felt so alive. At one point, I was shouting and heard him shushing me, so I closed my eyes and allowed my hand to rest on his beating heart.

Afterwards, he said, "Did you like that?"

"Yes, very much."

"Shall we meet again?"

"Yes."

Later, alone again in my room, I felt frightened: what if we had been discovered in the act? One moment, I never wanted to see Scott again; the next moment, I couldn't wait to see him. Our lovemaking couldn't be a sin, I reasoned: no one was hurt. In fact, two wounded soldiers were helped. We survived the war, and love was another reason to live. I believed this but the negative associations about homosexuals made known to me throughout my life and the Army rules and regulations had an effect: "What is to be my future? What am I good for?" I wrote in my war diary.

Yet, Scott and I found ways to be together. We golfed, went canoeing, rode bicycles, and in the evenings, by mutual consent, we made love in vacant rooms.

On August 14, 1945, President Harry S. Truman declared that the war was over. Soldiers and civilians—firemen, Red

Cross volunteers, and police—paraded down the street. Sirens sounded. American flags waved everywhere. Men and women embraced and kissed. I wanted to hug Scott, but I couldn't find him.

In October, Scott and I made love in a honeymoon suite. We opened the French doors and stood on the balcony overlooking the woods, fall foliage ablaze, feeling connected. In November we separated, never to see each other again.

HOME

On November 6, 1945, my mother, father, brother, and his wife, Jane, picked me up from my bus in Whitehall, New York. After hugs and handshakes, my father drove us home along Route 4 in Vermont.

"I'm so glad to have my boys home at last," Mother said.

"And a daughter-in-law," my father said through a smile.

"Yes," Mother said.

"She knows that she has married the Army," my brother said.

"And I'm willing to go wherever the Army sends us," Jane said enthusiastically.

My father turned on the radio. A lonely sounding accordion accompanied Marlene Dietrich singing "Lili Marlene." Numbness overcame me for a moment. My throat felt constricted. I swallowed air and began to sweat. Tears burned my eyes. I faced the window to conceal my emotion. Fair Haven and the Congregational Church came into view.

"How's Rev. Wells?" I asked.

"He's leaving us," mother said. "He's received a call to a church in Hollis, New York, where he grew up."

"I don't know how we're going to replace him," father said. "He was sure good to write you two boys while you were in the service."

"He sure was," I said, almost choking on the words, feeling the sting in my eyes again. "I hope we are going to see him before he leaves."

"You will," Mother said.

Soon we were pulling into the driveway. My father had all the leaves raked and firewood stacked neatly.

"Looks like you've been here all along," I said.

"Your dad has been working like a horse," Mother said.

"So has your mother," Father said.

The house was spotless. "You can put your duffel bag in our room," Mother said.

I walked into my parents' bedroom and dropped my bag. On Mother's dresser was a photograph of my father's parents, Samuel and Harriet Wood. We sat in the "Wood" pew at church. They were buried together in the town cemetery.

Beside the portrait of my father's parents was a photograph of Mother's parents, Joe and Mary Beard. I held the photograph, thinking about my childhood visits to see them in a section of New Castle, Pennsylvania called Mahoningtown, near the train yards. Grandpa Joe worked in a roundhouse where locomotives were stored and switched. He died before the war. Grandma Mary was in a nursing home. I placed the photograph back on the dresser and joined the others in the living room.

Mother, resembling her mother, was already wearing an apron to protect her dress while she sat between Harold and Jane, looking at their wedding pictures. My father, looking very much like Grandpa Joe in his ironed flannel shirt and creased trousers, was lifting a piece of wood from the brass bucket on the slate hearth to build a fire. One by one, I looked at Dad, Mother, Harold, and Jane, conscious of our being alive, and together. Thankful.

I scanned the room, mindful of the Windsor armchair and rocker, floorstand ashtray, a ship at sea painting hanging over the mantle, the radio, and the view to Birdseye Mountain through the picture window, so much a part of my father's retirement dreams.

"It all looks the same," I said.

"We're so glad to be back home," Mother said, "where your father can make a fire." Sparks and crackles sounded from the fireplace.

"Nothing beats the feel and smell of a wood fire," my father said.

Mother and Jane excused themselves to check on dinner. Already the familiar smells of Mother's cooking were filling the house.

Father, Harold, and I sat in the living room.

"How is married life treating you?" I asked Harold.

"So far, so good," he said. "We've been so busy visiting our family and friends, we haven't had much time for ourselves."

"You'll have plenty of time for that," Father said.

"The rest of our life," Harold replied.

"I can't believe I'm looking at the two of you," I said.

"I'm glad to say that war is just a memory now," Harold said.

"What memories come to mind?" I asked.

"There's not much to tell," he said. "We built roads and

moved supplies into the back door of China. We had a few air raids, but ours was mostly monotonous work."

"How does it feel to be retired, again?" Harold asked Father.

"I'm glad I don't have to make that trip to Springfield twice a week," he said. "There's plenty of work around here. The house could use a coat of paint."

Father poked the fire and sat back down.

"We almost lost you, though," Father said, looking at me. I couldn't speak. "We'll have much to be thankful for this Thanksgiving."

Soon we were sitting around the table. Father said grace, after which we ate pot roast and noodles. I can't remember before or since when food tasted so good. I awoke the next morning at my parent's home to some of my favorite smells: batter cooking in a waffle iron, Vermont maple syrup warming on the stove, coffee percolating and bacon sizzling in the skillet. Mother wanted to celebrate my first day of civilian life. She also ironed a sport shirt and pair of slacks for me.

After breakfast Harold and Jane left to make some visits, so I asked my father to drive me around Lake Bomoseen. The foliage season was over, the big hotels closed. The locals walked about town. Sugar maple leaves formed colorful mosaics on the ground. Although Dad had the car heater on, occasionally I would roll down the window, allowing the cold, crisp air to flow across my face.

"Not much has changed," Father said.

"So it seems. Except the flags."

Armed Forces service flags, with their blue and gold stars, hung in front of most homes. I noticed plenty of gold stars, which meant a serviceman had died. Seeing those stars, blue or gold, sparked more memories of blood and dead men lying motionless in mud.

My father asked, "Are you okay, son?"

"Sure," I said. "It's nothing."

When we pulled into our driveway back home, I noticed the two blue stars on my parent's service flag.

After lunch, Rev. Wells stopped by. Mother insisted we sit in the kitchen where she could serve coffee and cake and hear our conversations. Rev. Wells shook my hand.

"Get your medals, son," Dad said. "Show Rev. Wells your medals."

He seemed as proud of them as if they were his own. I obliged him.

"You must be very proud," Rev. Wells said to my father.

"Yes," my father said, biting his lip, looking away, and pulling a handkerchief out of his pocket to blow his nose.

"We thought we might lose him," Mother said.

"You couldn't get rid of me that easily," I said as I walked in with the medals.

"I'm proudest of this one," I said, pointing to the Combat Infantry Badge. "It's given only to Army Infantry who have fought on the front line."

Rev. Wells looked the medals over.

"What do we call you: captain, sergeant, or corporal?" he asked.

"Just call me mister," I replied.

"Well, mister, do you feel like preaching another sermon at your home church?"

"I've already told them about my Army days," I said. "I'm not sure what I could say."

"You'll find something to say," Mother said. "You're seldom at a loss for words."

"Pray," he said. "Ideas will come. I'll schedule you in January to give you plenty of time to prepare, and if you run into difficulties, just call."

"He'll have plenty of time," Father said. "He's a civilian now."

After Sunday worship, Harold and Jane left for Pittsburgh, and I moved into my old bedroom.

My second week home was filled with spontaneous visits from relatives, neighbors, and church members. Mother greeted them with cake and coffee. I talked about returning to college in January and thanked them for their prayers, cards, and visits. They kept their visits short, and I felt relieved when they left.

After the second week in Bomoseen I began to feel anxious and bored. I lacked patience. I didn't think much about the future or the past. I had to get out of the house and walk in the woods. What I would have given for a place to meet Scott, feel him, see him, have him feel me and see me. Make love. Guilt accompanied these thoughts. Yearning followed the guilt. Frustration followed the yearning. Eventually, I went home. I didn't exactly know what to do with myself. Life seemed suspended.

My mind kept drifting back to my Army life and war. By the end of the third week, I discovered a tentative calm, sitting on my parent's living room floor surrounded by photographs, VMail, maps of troop movements, French francs, Italian lira, newspaper clippings, and picture books from Camp Wolters and the Lake Placid Redistribution Center, which I pasted in an album as a way of holding on to military life—reconstructing it, reliving it. Mother had saved all my letters, so I included some of them as well. One letter stood out: Harold's attempt to supply Mother and Father with information about my condition after I had been wounded:

> February 29, 1944
>
> Captain H.N. Wood:
>
> I remember the night your brother was wounded. He was on outpost duty, challenged a group who turned out to be "Jerry," and they in turn fired at the "voice." A bullet hit him in his right chest and came out behind his shoulder blade. Wood, though wounded, manned his machine gun and drove off the Jerry patrol. Then he collapsed.

> We recommended him for the Silver Star. I don't know whether or not it went through, for I was wounded myself shortly thereafter, and have only just rejoined the company. His wound was serious, but not fatal. He will have a long period in the hospital. We will be glad to have him rejoin the company, for he is a fine type of boy. Incidentally Wood wasn't the least bit excited over his being wounded—took it as calmly as anyone I have ever seen. He wasn't in too much pain.
>
> *W.F. Loughman, First Lieutenant*

Later, mother, dusting the furniture around me, said, "Have you called Helen?"

"No, Mother."

She stopped polishing.

"Helen's awfully pretty, you know. She comes from a very nice family. She's a good, Christian girl. She'd make a good minister's wife."

"Mother, you're getting ahead of yourself," I said.

She walked over to me, put her hand on her hip.

"If you wait to become engaged until you are out of college, Helen may find somebody else," she said. "If you two are serious, maybe you ought not wait so long. Just because you get engaged doesn't mean you have to get married right away."

"Please, mother. I'm trying to concentrate," I said, arranging another page of war memories, thinking about how my parents had expected me to follow my brother into the Boy Scouts, the University of Pennsylvania, and the Army. He could do no wrong, I thought, and just because he married Jane, Mother expected me to become engaged to a girl I hardly knew. What would it take to please her?

That night, after I said my prayers, I slept and dreamed. Shadowy figures lurked behind trees. Dream figures floated like Halloween masks—sinister, grinning, bloody, and screaming. I heard human screams, explosions, and felt the cramped feeling of being in the foxhole. These images floated in and out of my consciousness with changing intensity: they threatened to smother me at times. I felt myself being pulled down. I woke up shaking and sweaty, rubbing the scar on my chest, and quietly and tearfully asked God to help me.

Thanksgiving came. Harold and Jane were visiting from Pittsburgh, discussing Harold's discharge and their plans to move to Lorain, Ohio. I had just taken a bite of Mother's pumpkin pie.

"Have you given any thought to what you might give Helen for Christmas?" she asked.

"I haven't the slightest idea. Do you have any suggestions?"

"Maybe she would like an engagement ring?"

I capitulated. The following week, Mother helped me pick out a ring at Parker and Son's Jewelers, located on the town square in Fair Haven. I wrapped it, insured it, and mailed it. On Christmas morning, our telephone rang. It was Helen.

"What a beautiful ring. I just love it. I'm accepting it. I'll be happy to be your bride. Yes. Yes. Yes." She made kissing sounds over the telephone, and said, "Oh Bob. I love you so much."

Helen was happy. Helen's parents were happy. My parents were happy. Harold and Jane, visiting at Christmas, were happy. Everybody congratulated me. I allowed myself to embrace the idea of marriage. I dreamed of becoming a husband, envisioning children on my knee, fatherhood. I could see my family sitting on the same pew in church each Sunday and parishioners adoring them.

For months, I continued a relationship with Helen through correspondence, although my heart was not in it. Eventually, detecting my lack of enthusiasm for our wedding and the absence of a physical spark, she broke off our engagement.

If I could speak with Helen now, I would say, "Helen, I do not know what has become of you. You thoughtfully wrote letters to me when I was a soldier in a faraway place. You were kind enough to accept my proposal for marriage. I didn't know then that I possessed the capacity to bring such joy to another human being. I can only imagine your expectation, wondering if my behavior would ever match my words of affection. How disappointed you must have been. I thank God for your insight and rejection of my proposal. I regret any pain my limited self-awareness may have caused you to suffer. Forgive me."

Returning to School

In January 1946, taking advantage of the GI Bill, I returned to the University of Pennsylvania.

Discussions with a dean about my promise to serve God prompted a change in my major from journalism to religious journalism. I became a "heeler" for the *Daily Pennsylvanian*, our student newspaper. English courses, the bulk of my school load, required much reading and writing.

Most of my free time was spent at the Christian Association where I could eat delicious but inexpensive lunches, play chess or ping pong, sit and read, or meet with friends. My friends were mostly veterans with whom I could talk of military life and war. One day, I sat with an amputee, a burn victim, a head wound, and another chest wound, exchanging stories about ambush, artillery, foul weather, guard duty, combat, escapades on leave, military hospitals, nurses, and romance. The amputee boasted about killing. Every dead German was a trophy to him, and he confessed to looting and raping innocent bystanders.

"I wonder if God forgives us?" I asked.

"Who cares?" the burn victim answered angrily. "Where was God when the war started? Where was God when my friends were being blown to hell?"

His scorched cheek, covered with scars resembling chicken's feet, reddened as he shouted, "Don't talk to me about God!"

As the burn victim shouted over the loss of his comrades, I wept. Looking back, I think his anger and my quiet tears were probably the same emotion, his let loose on the world, mine turned inward, drowning my heart. I didn't blame God for the war; I blamed Hitler. Yet, I couldn't argue with the angry man: I, too, had felt abandoned by God in combat. Instead, embarrassed by the tears, I stared at the floor for a while and then walked away.

A chaplain, an older man with gray hair and a kind face, spoke to me from his office doorway.

"I see you were a soldier."

"Yes. I'm just back," I said, wiping my eyes.

"I fought in the first one."

"So did my father. In what branch did you serve?"

"I was a chaplain in the Army."

"My dad was Army," I said. "Coast artillery."

"Come, sit. You don't mind talking to a Lutheran, do you?"

"Not at all."

He motioned for me to sit in a chair beside his desk, and he sat behind it.

"Where were you?" he asked.

"In Italy with the Thirty-Sixth Division."

My eyes burned with another load of tears as I told him about my experience.

"God only knows why I lived when so many didn't. I'm thinking God must have a mission for me, so I've promised my life to God's service."

"That's quite a commitment."

"Fulfilling that promise makes life worth living."

"I see," he said. "So how are you coping?"

"Coping?"

"Handling the aftermath."

"I try not to think about things too much. My dad told me that too much thinking leads to depression. 'Keep busy' is his motto."

"And how do you keep busy?"

"Besides my schoolwork, I help at the paper. On Sundays, I go to church."

"Where?"

"I've attended Presbyterian, Episcopal, and Baptist churches. I've even tried a Catholic Church."

"Why so many?"

"I'm not sure. The sermons: I've heard the classics quoted a lot but very little about the rebuilding of Europe, VA hospitals, or MacArthur's rule in Japan. Also, I haven't felt welcomed by any of the parishioners."

"Then why do you go?"

"Habit. To get church bulletins to send to my mother, to thank God, and to pray."

"And what do you pray?"

"I pray for those who are still recovering from combat wounds, for the dead, for loved ones left behind and for myself, that I prove worthy of life."

Tears spilled out of my burning eyes. I swallowed and looked down at the floor, unable to speak. I thought about my prayers for soldiers detained in stockades with "Q"'s written on their backs and Scott, and wondered how the Lutheran chaplain might react to such prayers. I didn't risk mentioning them.

"I'm not sure any of us is worthy," he said. "Most of us are glad for grace and forgiveness. Remember that."

"Thanks. I will," I said, standing. "I have a class to attend."

He invited me to return after class to meet the Baptist chaplain, Fred Igler, who was working on an outreach program.

"I think he'll be interested in your story," the chaplain said.

The Rev. Dr. Fred Igler, a short, stocky, businesslike man, vigorously shook my hand. "I'm not going to waste your time Wood, so I'll get right to the point," he said. "We're seeking students to represent the University and the CA through deputations—speaking before youth groups throughout the city."

"What do students speak about?"

"Students usually speak on broad subjects such as pacifism, the postwar generation, or the labor movement. They're sent in pairs, so no student bears the total speaking responsibility. We try to select students with complementary ideas or speeches."

"Did you have a topic in mind for me?"

"As a veteran, I thought you might offer young people insight into the soldier's life and faith."

Deputations, like preaching at my home church, seemed like a practical way to serve God, I thought, and the Lutheran pastor and Dr. Igler were friendly enough, like big brothers. I felt they really cared about me.

"Can we count on you?" Igler asked.

"Sure," I said.

Two weeks later, I stood before fifteen junior and senior high school students in a small Baptist church in east Philadelphia. Their young, eager faces seemed fixed on my partner speaking about his work in alternate services as a firefighter in National Parks. After his deputation I talked about the team effort required in combat. A question-and-answer session followed in which several children reminisced about family members who served in the war.

"What do you think happens to soldiers killed in war?" one young fellow asked me.

A scene from a British war movie came to mind: soldiers wearing different uniforms riding an escalator from earth to heaven.

"They'll go to heaven on an escalator," I answered, without thought. "Good people get there quicker, but since God loves us all, everyone will get there eventually. I believe everyone killed in war has found peace with God."

I'm sure I would not make such a statement today, having had the benefit of a theological education and years of experience in church life. Perhaps I would offer a few words about the redemptive aspects of sacrifice. In that moment of social isolation processing the aftermath of war, keeping busy with purpose helped me. Hopefully, it helped others.

An Opening Up

One day, as a reporter for the paper, I was sent to College Hall. The room was crammed with 200 men listening to a guest lecturer. To fit in the room, we sat very close to one another. Beside me sat a man wearing a sailor's uniform. His short, blond hair was neatly combed, his round, gentle face clean-shaven. I stared at him. His blue eyes met mine several times, and, as the professor lectured, the man beside me gradually allowed his knee to rest on mine.

He smiled at me. I smiled back. I knew he knew. I wrote my name and campus address beside my notes. On his notes, he wrote, "Jimmy. I live off campus."

After the lecture I introduced myself, extending my hand. Jimmy took it, and said, "Pleased to meet you."

"Likewise," I said.

"Good lecture," he said.

"Yes," I said.

He suddenly began to look around the room, his face wrinkled with a worried expression. People behind us were waiting, so we joined the flow of students leaving the room. I lost track of him. I searched for him without success, and walked back to my dorm room, alone. I thought about Jimmy's firm handshake, the electric feeling of his knee against mine, his smile, and his apparent warmth. I also thought about his Navy uniform and the rules and regulations of military life.

Weeks later, I saw him in his Navy blues, sitting in the student union, reading a book. I had just finished an interview for the newspaper and had a few hours to kill before my broadcast at the campus radio station.

"You look great in your uniform," I said.

Glancing up from his book, Jimmy blushed.

"ROTC," he said, then continued to read. He looked preoccupied, but then a smile broke over his face.

"I remember you," he said, staring into my eyes.

"Do you have some time on your hands?" I asked, boldly.

Jimmy glanced at his watch, cocked his head, and sheepishly said, "What do you have in mind?"

"I have a private room."

"Why not?" he said. "I've always wanted to see the inside of a dorm room."

On the short walk from the student union to the dormitory, Jimmy said how much he envied the students on campus, and how much time he spent commuting.

"Nice room," he said. "Does the university supply all this furniture?" he asked, folding his shirt and draping it over the back of a chair.

"Most of it," I said, throwing off my clothes, unconcerned where they fell.

Naked, I sat on the bed, watching Jimmy match his trouser cuffs, fold their leg creases over his arm, and drape them over the chair next to his shirt. He turned and stood before me. I wrapped my arms around his waist and pulled him on top of me, wrapping my legs in his. Kneeling over him, I kissed his neck, shoulders, nipples, and stomach. Jimmy then embraced me and pressed his lips against mine, sending his tongue deep into my mouth. We made love.

Then from my bed I watched him wash himself at the sink in my room and dress. He glanced at his watch and gathered his books.

"I have a train to catch," he said.

"When do I see you again?"

Between his commuting and ROTC duties and my work with the radio and newspaper, we had an hour available between us on Thursday nights.

"I'll see you next week," he said as he was leaving. He had been in my room about ten minutes.

The following Thursday, Jimmy promptly arrived, and we made love again. He asked about my scars and about my parents. We were together for half an hour that evening. At our next meeting he gave me a black-and-white photograph of himself smiling and wearing a University of Pennsylvania t-shirt. I had the picture framed and placed it on my desk. That Thanksgiving he invited me to his home in Swarthmore.

Jimmy's home, in many ways, resembled my childhood home in Lorain. It was comfortable, nicely furnished, neat, clean, and homey. Jimmy's mother and younger sister worked in the kitchen while Jimmy and I sat with his father, who had the presence of a professor—staid and academic, smoking a pipe, asking questions about my classes and campus life. He was impressed that I was named the historian for the class of 1948.

Later, around an elegantly set dinner table, we paused for a moment of silence. Jimmy's father carved and served the turkey. The rest of us politely passed around mash potatoes, dressing, and cranberry sauce. Throughout dinner, Jimmy smiled a lot, which made me feel welcomed.

"Bring your young friend any time," Jimmy's mother said as I left.

Jimmy walked with me to the train station. Waiting for the train, I wanted to hug him but neither one of us would permit such a physical gesture in public. I told him how much I had enjoyed meeting his family and the homecooked meal. When my train arrived, I shook his hand and thanked him again.

After Christmas break, we resumed our Thursday night trysts. We both spoke of the "release" we felt. By early March, Jimmy began to make excuses for why he couldn't meet me. Then one night in April, we met for dinner. After we had eaten, I stood up, thinking we would go back to my room, as was our habit, but Jimmy hesitated.

"Would it be okay with you if we didn't have sex?" he said. "I'm not sure I am comfortable with that aspect of our relationship."

"I thought we were getting along splendidly," I said, trying to cover up the rejection I felt.

"You'll be graduating in a few months," he said.

"So?" I responded.

"We need to meet new people," he said. "Have you gone about meeting people in Philadelphia?"

"I haven't. I don't go to bars because I don't drink."

"I don't care for bars either," he said, "but I've met men in Rittenhouse Square. I'll show you."

Reluctantly, I agreed to meet him there.

Around Rittenhouse Square, uniformed doormen stood in front of apartment buildings—five and six stories high, with awnings out to the street. Cement walks from opposite corners of the square met in the center where a small fountain dripped layers of water. Park benches and gas lights lined the walks. When we arrived, most of the men walking in the square looked to be businessmen returning home from a busy day at the office. At sunset the gas lights glowed. Fewer people walked the square. Soon an older man dressed in a blazer with a gold watch chain dangling from his vest pocket walked in our direction; he glanced at us as he passed.

"He's one," Jimmy said.

A few minutes later, another older man with a stiff posture, wearing a suit and tie walked towards us. He stared me in the eye as he walked by.

"He's one."

We spotted at least fifteen men Jimmy thought were homosexual. Most were older.

"If you want to meet someone, you have to be alone," he said.

The following week, dressed in jeans and an open shirt, I returned to Rittenhouse Square at dusk and sat on a bench. Soon, a man walked by, stopped, turned, walked back towards me, and put his foot up on the bench.

"Do you have a light?" he asked.

"I don't smoke."

"What else don't you do?"

"I don't date women."

"How about men?"

"Where are you going in such a hurry?" I asked.

"I'm late for a party at that apartment house there," he said, pointing. "Would you like to join me?"

"Sure," I said, curious to know what kind of party he might be attending, open to where the night might lead.

"I'm Phillip," he said as we entered the apartment building.

"I'm Bob," I said.

"What brings you to Philadelphia?" he asked on the elevator.

"I'm a student at the university," I said.

The elevator stopped on the fourth floor, and Phillip led me down a plush carpeted corridor to a door, which opened soon after he rang the doorbell. A man old enough to be my father answered the door, and said, "Who's your friend?" to Phillip as we entered.

"Bob from Penn," Phillip replied.

"Do make yourself at home, Bob," he said, and whispered something into Phillip's ear. They laughed.

"Excuse me, Bob," Phillip said. "I see a friend with whom I need to speak. Wait for me by the French doors across the way."

Crossing the room, I admired oriental carpets, antiques, paintings, sculpture, porcelain figurines, draperies, and chandeliers. I had never seen such luxurious decor. Everything looked fragile, breakable, and expensive.

Older men in coats and ties, in groups of three or four, drank cocktails, ate hors d'oeuvres off fine china, and talked. One of the men approached me.

"Are you a student at Penn?" he said. "I thought I recognized you from campus. I teach at the dental college. How did you happen to come to our gathering tonight?"

"I came with Phillip."

"Be careful, young man: Do you know who Phillip's father is?"

"No, we just met in the square."

"You should," he said, leading me by the arm onto the balcony overlooking the square. "He's a gangster."

"Really?

"Attention everybody. Attention," the elder host said. "Tonight happens to be Felix's and Jacques' fifth anniversary. Happy anniversary," he said, lifting a glass of champagne. "Happy, happy."

"Happy, happy," several men said at once, lifting their glasses.

"Five years is a long time," I said to the dentist.

"Your host and his lover have been together for more than thirty-five years," he replied. I had no idea that men could be couples for such a long time.

"Really?" I said, "Do all these men have partners?"

The dentist pointed again.

"See him?" he whispered. "He is the local commissioner, and over there is his lover: I think he's in real estate. Hands off: they are strictly monogamous. And that one is on the staff of the Museum of Fine Arts. His lover, the one talking to the commissioner, is a famous radio personality. They have an open relationship, an understanding; they sleep around, but always come home. But of course, Bob, this is all very confidential. Once we leave this party no one remembers who or what he saw. Goodness, what reputations could be ruined."

"I understand," I said, amazed by the types of relationships he had described.

"But now I must mingle," he said, leaving me alone to survey the scene.

Everyone seemed so sophisticated and successful, like celebrities. I felt inadequate among them. I knew nothing about art or antiques. The only traveling I had done was in the Army. Besides, I was attracted to men my own age. Ten minutes more, observing and listening, and I headed for the door.

"Do come again, whoever you are," I heard someone say as I left the party.

I thought about men sharing long-term relationships like my parents. I wanted such a relationship, but somehow, I knew I wouldn't find him in Rittenhouse Square.

As for Jimmy, he became a priest in the Episcopal Church and remained one of my closest friends.

Consequence

Back on campus, Dr. Igler invited me to join a pre-theological class—a support group for students planning to attend seminary. I was curious about how others addressed concerns about the vocation of ministry, and I wanted more information about seminaries. Instead, I heard debates about labor unions, race relations, and welfare. The war was seldom mentioned, perhaps because I was the only veteran in the group. Besides Igler, the only other person I knew was a student named Willard, with whom I had worked on Christian Association fund-raising drives and deputations.

Igler allowed the group to run itself. In one of the meetings, after an opening prayer, a student said, "Tonight, I'd like to discuss the subject of homosexuality. As far as I am concerned, homosexuality is a sin."

I cringed, half expecting him to point his finger at me.

"Turn to Leviticus 18:22," he said, opening his King James version of the Bible, and pompously reading, "'Thou shalt not lie with mankind as with womankind: it is abomination.' An abomination is a vile, shameful habit." Leviticus 20:13 describes the consequences of such acts: "If a man also lies with mankind as he lieth with a woman, both of them have committed an abomination; they shall surely be put to death; their blood shall be upon them."

I scribbled down these chapters and verses, heretofore unfamiliar to me. Hearing them had felt like a personal attack, but I couldn't defend myself. Protesting such thoughts might cause them to think that I was a homosexual. I stared at Igler, hoping he would explain the words away. Silence. I looked at Willard. Silence. Another student insisted we all turn to Romans 1:24–27, and read:

> Wherefore God also gave them up to uncleanness through the lusts of their own hearts, to dishonour their own bodies between themselves: Who changed the truth of God into a lie, and worshipped and served the creature more than the Creator, who is blessed for ever. Amen. For this cause God gave them up unto vile affections: for even their women did change the natural use into that which is against nature: And likewise also the men, leaving the natural use of the woman, burned in their lust one toward another; men with men working that which is unseemly, and receiving in themselves that recompence of their error which was meet.

Back in my dorm room I looked up these verses, feeling betrayed in a way. Since childhood I had been instructed about

God's love, which unconditionally included me. Jesus wanted me to belong to Him, wanted to be my friend, and I thought he was. Yet, the more I read, the more confused I became. I didn't feel like an abomination. I hadn't given up relations with women; I hadn't had any. But it seemed that these texts were clearly condemning what I had enjoyed with Scott and Jimmy. Maybe I was a sinner, but I didn't feel like a sinner.

During another pre-theological meeting, a student read the story of Jesus walking on the water.

"Was Jesus divine?" one of them asked.

"Of course," another said.

"Did he really walk on top of the water?"

"The Bible says it, so it's true."

Again, those defending the miracle seemed certain about their opinions, which they presented as facts. Igler listened quietly, offering no rebuttal. I didn't know whether he agreed with the other students, or if he was a neutral third party. I knew I didn't agree.

"In my opinion," I said hesitantly, "this story depicts Jesus risking his own life to show concern for friends: it only appeared to the disciples that he had gotten there by walking on the water. Walking on the water is not as important as Jesus' caring."

"You don't know what you are talking about, Wood," a student insisted. "When did you come to know the Lord as your Savior?"

I didn't answer. Other students recited exact dates, places, and even the method of their salvation.

"Salvation," one of the students preached, "is the only evidence of truly belonging to the church."

I couldn't point to a single day or event in my life that would have constituted my salvation in their terms. My experiences of God were inspired moments: the love I received from family, church members, and friends; my experience of God as a twelve-year-old; beauty in nature; courage in battle; and hope in recovery from wounds. God had been with me through the "valley of the shadow of death," and inspired a purpose for my life. I hoped for some validation from Igler or Willard, but they remained quiet.

"Are you saved, Bob?" the student asked again.

"I wouldn't use that term," I replied.

"If you don't know, then you are not."

"How can you think about going to a seminary if you are not even saved?"

"I plan to study religious journalism, not church work," I said. "But don't you worry, I've experienced God in my life."

"That's not the same as being saved."

My red-lettered King James Bible given to me for perfect Sunday School attendance, which contained words inspired by God, assuring me of love, reminding me of life, was now being used as a tool of condemnation and judgment. I didn't know what to say, and, again, looked to Igler to challenge these thoughts. Igler showed no awareness or concern about my frustration, but, surprisingly, after the session he asked me which seminary I planned to attend.

"I'm thinking about Oberlin, I grew up near Oberlin," I said.

"Oberlin's a fine school," Igler said. "I know Dean Graham at Oberlin. We're good friends. Would you like me to write you a letter of recommendation?"

I was surprised when Igler wrote a letter on my behalf. I felt grateful and reassured. Igler must have seen something in me worthy of respect.

When I received the short, official acceptance from Oberlin, I felt pride in the accomplishment and joy that my goal to serve God was being realized. I phoned home with the news, and my parents were thrilled.

Frustrated by the narrow scope of the conversations and tired of having my thoughts ignored by the other students, I stopped attending the pre-theological group.

Later, while walking across campus, Willard hailed me.

"Why have you stopped coming to the group?"

"I don't find it supportive or helpful."

"But you still want to go to a seminary?" he asked, walking beside me.

"Yes."

"Why?"

"To serve God and gain some understanding about an issue that I feel the church is ignoring," I said.

"What do you mean?"

"I have difficulty talking about it. It's kind of personal. Can you keep a secret?"

"Sure."

I do not know why I chose that moment to speak to that person. Perhaps I wanted someone to understand my point of view, and I thought Willard was a friend. I stopped walking and faced him.

"Well, I'm a homosexual and as a homosexual I'm finding little understanding from religion."

Willard didn't flinch.

"A friend of my brother was also a homo," Willard said. "And my brother continued to be his friend after finding out. But if you ask me, all you need is a date with a pretty girl. If you would go to bed with one pretty girl, you'd be cured."

"I was engaged to a pretty girl and didn't feel a thing."

"Maybe she was the wrong girl."

"Maybe we can talk about it another time but keep it to yourself, okay? I must get to a staff meeting for the yearbook."

"Okay," he said. "I won't tell a soul."

Several days later Dr. Igler sent a message demanding I come to his office. I thought he had a new deputation assignment or more news from Oberlin; but he looked agitated when I entered his office.

"I wrote a letter to Dean Graham on your behalf," he said. "Dean Graham and I have known each other for twenty years."

His tone was serious, angry.

"Are you a homosexual?" he asked.

I felt my face redden and my legs become weak. I almost lost my breath.

"Answer me. Are you a homosexual?"

I couldn't speak. Confidence and trust didn't mean much to Willard.

"Don't bother, I know," he said. "Why didn't you tell me that you were a queer? I would never have written a letter of recommendation for you if I had known."

He became more and more disturbed as I fought back panic.

"So, you're a queer?" he said and looked at me with disgust.

I stuttered something to indicate that I was one.

"Have you had sexual relations with other students on campus?"

"Yes."

"Do you realize young man, that a clergyman such as myself must be symbol of virtue and moral correctness? Do you understand the position you've put me in?"

I felt defenseless.

"You've taken advantage of my friendship," he said. "You've been dishonest. You certainly have not behaved as a Christian gentleman."

I remained speechless.

"You write Dean Graham and tell him, or I promise, I will. And tell him of your dishonesty. Write him and tell him that you are a queer, and if he still wants to accept you, that's his decision."

I left Igler's office wondering who else knew. I felt like a cornered rabbit or a scolded child—dry mouthed, pathetic, caught like an animal in a trap, pulling, increasing my pain, dead and alive at the same time, life slipping away. I prayed faith would kick in, but my heart continued to explode within my chest. There were no bombs or guns now, just power exercised to diminish, exclude, and humiliate. Finally, I submitted.

I was in shock. I thought that everyone must know. My brain churned through consequences. My parents knew of my plans to attend the seminary in the fall. I had been accepted and now Igler was threatening to have me rejected. Everything was over, I thought. I felt ashamed, as if I had failed creation itself. I went to my room and began to write through tears that I engaged in homosexual relations with other students but also expressing that I felt the Lord had called me to serve in the church.

Two weeks later, Dean Graham's reply came.

"Dear Mr. Wood, come as planned," he wrote. "We'll talk about your problem when you arrive."

Sanatorium

Soon after I wrote the letter to Graham, I opened a letter from my mother. I was expecting to read about my parents' recent church activities, their neighbors dropping in for coffee, or news about my brother and his wife and their new baby. Instead, my mother was deeply concerned about my father, who had become nervous, on edge, and sometimes incommunicative. He was no longer able to drive and wouldn't be able to attend my graduation. He would see a specialist soon. I offered to come home before graduation, but she told me it would only make him distraught if I didn't graduate on time.

After commencement I said brief but heartfelt goodbyes to fellow editors at *The Daily Pennsylvanian*, then boarded the train home.

Back home father sat in his easy chair with the floorstand ashtray close by. Physically, he looked the same as he always had. Mother had him wearing his flannel shirt and cotton trousers, neatly ironed. His shoes were shined, and his hair was combed, not a hair out of place.

"Hi, Dad," I said.

"Hello," he answered. No smile. No handshake. No gesture to stand up to greet me. No gladness to see me.

"I'm a college graduate. Would you like to see my diploma?" I said, hoping for a little joy.

"Sure," he said, flatly.

Proudly, I handed him my degree. He held it for a moment before looking at it.

"Congratulations," he said quietly, without much feeling. I thought he was going to smile but he just stared with a confused expression on his face. He started to say something but stopped, as if trying to recall words to say. He blankly stared at me for a while, and softly said, "You did it." Again, I thought he might smile, but he stared without expression. More seconds ticked off before he said, "Be sure to show it to your mother." His expression remained vacant. A minute later, he said, without animation, "You did it."

"Hopefully, I'll have another one to show you in three years," I said, as Mother walked in and stood behind Father. "How are you feeling?"

"Tired. They won't let me do anything."

"Are you getting outside, taking walks, playing with the dog?"

"Yes."

Behind him, Mother shook her head, no.

"Bob," Mother said. "Why don't you talk to your dad again in the morning. He's very tired."

After she helped my father to bed, she confided in me: "I'm so frustrated with our doctor: all he can say is that your father is having some kind of breakdown," she said. "He says that we'll know more when the specialist sees him."

In the weeks that followed, the expression on father's face remained blank. Personality had left his eyes. He no longer had his sense of humor. He would start to do something—empty the trash or pick up the mail—and then forget what he set out to do. Several times, I discovered him wandering around outdoors as if he couldn't find his way back to the house. He was never violent or belligerent, just docile and lost looking. Sometimes he would sit alone in the car, smoking. Seeing him there was a pitiful sight.

My father worked for years to provide food, clothing, and shelter for us, and money for my education. He had been our family's bulwark in matters of faith, saying the blessings at our table and encouraging us in our spiritual lives. He had been to war. He was a man whose approval I sought, who had been so proud of my achievements as a scout, soldier, and student. Seeing him looking beaten down, defeated, and without vitality saddened me deeply. I was not surprised when the specialist recommended that Mother commit him to a sanatorium in Brattleboro, Vermont, what many called "the crazy house."

Our neighbor drove us to Brattleboro. I rode up front, and Mother and Father took the back seat.

"You're going to get the help you need," Mother said. "So, you needn't worry about me, I'll be just fine. Bob will be around to help."

Father sat beside her, quiet, without comment or complaint.

I silently wondered what might have caused his condition and was seized with fear that Dr. Igler might have spoken with him about me.

We drove for about an hour when the sanatorium, a four-story brick building surrounded by a spacious, green lawn, came into view. The grounds looked serene but the building rather severe. I noticed the windows were barred. Several older men wearing casual clothes accompanied by women in white coats were walking outside.

Mother and I accompanied father as far as the reception room, where she signed documents and a doctor conferred with us.

"Our treatment will require a complete break from family and familiar surroundings since they might be the cause of the patient's condition," he said. "We've noticed relapses when patients receive mail, so we discourage writing. You will receive weekly reports, and of course, his doctor can visit at any time. Try not to worry, we'll look after Mr. Wood, now."

Mother walked over to father who showed no emotion or concern. She took a deep breath, as if holding in her feelings, and kissed him on the cheek.

"You'll be home soon, dear," she said.

An orderly took Father's arm, picked up his suitcase, and led him away from us. Mother and I both cried.

"You did the right thing, Mother," I said on the way home. "Do you have any idea what might have brought this on?"

"Not a clue."

"You really had no choice," said our neighbor.

Mother cried again, and I held her hand.

"We'll just have to leave him in God's hands," Mother said.

"Yes," I said, "We'll all pray."

"And get on with our lives the best way we can," Mother said. "I'll learn what I need to learn."

"And I'll get my driver's license."

"That'll be a help when you are home on the weekends."

Mother knew I had taken a job working at camp for six weeks to earn money for seminary. The following week, I got my driver's license and began work at Camp OWanYaKa. Mother and I spent weekends together.

For many weeks the news from the sanatorium remained the same: not much change in his condition. Around the table and before we went to sleep each night, we prayed for his healing. On Sundays our minister and all the praying members of our congregation prayed for him. Through prayer our hope for his recovery increased. God would act, we thought. After a month our family doctor told mother that father's health was improving, so she announced at church that our prayers were being answered. I rejoiced.

The night before I was to leave to start Oberlin Seminary, Mother told me Father would be coming home. His doctor had advised that I shouldn't delay my departure. He also warned that I shouldn't refer to my father's illness in my letters or phone conversations.

Seeing Mother standing alone in the driveway touched me. The rule maker, the home organizer and cleaner, the one who had shown the emotions in our family would be greeting her sick husband soon. Although she had been alone on weekdays during the war and had done nothing to encourage dependence, I felt protective of her. Perhaps I was feeling the security of family disappear.

I hoped my upcoming conversations with the dean at Oberlin about the Igler affair wouldn't create more problems. I vowed never to discuss Igler or my sexual problem with my father.

"Please God," I prayed as I drove towards Ohio. "Keep Dad safe. Let him be well. And forgive me my many sins."

Seminary

In August of 1948, I drove along a flat, straight Ohio state highway past corn fields, farm stands, small community churches, and restaurants. The highway remained straight and flat on into Oberlin, where cross streets intersecting it at regular intervals marked square residential blocks, beyond which a business district began. I drove by two banks, a movie house, a bus station, several clothing stores, a real estate office, and three churches before reaching Tappan Square in the center of town.

Tall trees shaded walkways leading to various parts of Oberlin College, which surrounded the square. At one end of the square stood the great stone arch commemorating missionaries from Oberlin killed during the Boxer Rebellion in China. The administration office, I knew from an admission letter I had received, was nearby. I had made up my mind to speak to Dean Graham immediately.

However, when I visited his office, I discovered that he had left Oberlin. Dean Stidley had taken his place. So, the dreaded conversation never happened. When I left the dean's office, I whispered to myself, "Thank you, God." I vowed to put sex out of my mind and study hard to make good grades. No one need know about my sex life.

The seminary, four stone buildings set apart from the college, surrounded a courtyard. In one of the buildings, I found my dorm room, a divided square, each half furnished with a bed, bureau, bookcase, and desk. My roommate had not arrived, so I chose a bed, made it, then put away my clothes and school supplies. Afterwards, I roamed the halls, helping other students move in.

Twenty students comprised the junior class. Half of them were veterans. By the third week, I knew most of the students by their first names and which ones were veterans. As had been the case in college and the Army, I felt as if I was the only homosexual there. I spent what little free time I had in the company of veterans, particularly those who experienced combat.

My reading and understanding of the Bible changed. Before, I had read the Bible in a devotional, unquestioning manner, hoping to learn about God through some sort of magical revelation. Trying to connect the ancient words directly to the circumstances of modern life was sometimes confusing. At Oberlin I discovered the scripture's complexities through my research and questions: To whom were the authors of the Old and New Testament writing and why? What problems in ancient Israel's tribal league or the monarchy or the early church were being addressed through the various writings? Did similar problems exist today? How did God relate to human beings through covenant? What did God promise the ancient community of believers and leaders? What did God expect from them? Who was Jesus? What was accomplished through his life and death? Exegesis—the interpretation of scripture—required sorting out the historical contexts and styles of the various biblical authors before making applications of the words to modern life.

I was compelled by the scripture lessons on justice, warnings against nationalistic pride that took the place of faith in God, and a love offered to all, unconditionally. I applied my lessons to anti-German and anti-Japanese sentiments prevalent in our culture at the time, race relations, the plight of migrant workers, unemployed or disabled veterans, and, privately, homosexuals.

In an Introduction to Church History course, I learned how the church evolved beyond the pages of the Bible, about the power struggles between secular and church leaders, church schisms, reformations, and the development of modern denominations and church polity. Spiritual ideas, when fueled by unexamined conviction, could be revolutionary and dangerous, I learned. People were imprisoned, even killed, for their beliefs. I began to think in more deliberate ways about what I believed.

Walter Horton, my professor of theology, assigned us to write about our experience of God. I recalled lessons about God from Sunday school: how God had created the world and the people of the world and had shown love for the people of the world by sending Jesus to live and die for their sins, and how God hears and answers the prayers of believers.

I wrote about my parents' faith, their church attendance and offerings, grace at the table, and their love. I remembered my vision of God assuring me of long life when I was twelve years old, and how during confirmation I had been taught that Jesus wanted to be my friend. I wrote about feeling God with me and protecting me in combat and during my recuperation, about how unworthy I had felt to be alive when so many of my comrades had died, and about my promise to dedicate my life to God through journalism. I recounted the times I felt God had answered prayers. My notions of God expanded when reading theologians like Augustine, Aquinas, Luther, Calvin, Barth, and Brunner, whose ideas about God were organized in systematic ways.

I found Karl Barth's writings particularly meaningful. As professor of theology in Bonn, Germany during Hitler's rise to power, Barth emphasized God's sovereignty. The Kingdom of God, to Barth, existed beyond human thought, control, or manipulation, and was realized through God's incomprehensible love. Through Jesus, the Holy Spirit, and the Church, God's love could be known and felt. By experiencing that love, one entered the Kingdom of God.

As I read Barth's work, I imagined him writing to encourage anxious parishioners in Germany not to exchange their faith in God for faith in the Third Reich. God's love was available despite the capriciousness of life, I thought. After combat, my father's illness, and the Igler affair, reading Barth's words about God's love affected me deeply. If God loved me, I reasoned, he loved me as I was.

Homiletics, the art of sermon construction and delivery, was my first Practical Theology course. I was surprised when my professor said that among the list of relevant sermon topics was sex. "After all, most church members are not celibate or eunuchs," he said. I reasoned that his words about sex meant heterosexual sex, normal sex. We practiced our sermons in class and chapel services, and then we were sent out to preach in rural churches.

These churches, unlike churches I had attended in Lorain, Fair Haven, and Philadelphia, were poorer, with fewer members—from as few as seven members to as many as thirty. Worship in these churches was informal. Pianos instead of organs accompanied the hymns. Soloists, not choirs, sang special music. Parishioners announced church news and prayer concerns through long, rambling announcements. They prayed long, heartfelt prayers. In some cases, worship lasted for several hours.

Sunday after Sunday, I preached the latest theology and biblical research and timely quotations from contemporary church leaders while strange men and women yawned and coughed, babies cried, and young children wiggled in their pews.

During Christmas vacation, I drove out to a small farming community east of Oberlin, and found my assigned church, a rectangle built of cinder blocks surrounded by pickup trucks.

"You must be Bob Wood," a burly middle-aged man said as I entered the church. "I'm Raymond Floyd. People call me Ray. I'm a deacon here, and my job is to lead the worship service. I'll introduce you, and then you are on your own."

He extended his hand. I shook it and felt power in his grip.

"We appreciate you coming," he said, handing me a hymnal.

"Do you have a church bulletin?" I asked.

"Nope. You'll have to follow along like everybody else. And afterwards you'll be joining my wife and me and our kids for Sunday dinner."

We walked to the front of the church, and Ray pointed to a spot on the front pew where I sat. Ray stood behind a small lectern.

"Welcome to the house of the Lord," Ray said. "Let us pray. Our preacher this morning is a first-year student at Oberlin, Bob Wood. Please make him welcome."

We stood and sang "Onward Christian Soldiers," sat down, and Ray, listing them by name, prayed for the sick and housebound. We sang another hymn, Ray sat down, and I stood and placed my Bible, hymnal, Concordance, and my sermon notes on the small lectern. After the last verse, I began to preach. When I came to the point in my sermon when I had planned to read from the Concordance, it slid off the lectern and landed flat and hard on the wooden floor. Embarrassed, I walked around the lectern and down several steps to retrieve the large book, as the congregation laughed. When I returned to the lectern, I couldn't find the page from which I wanted to read because the bookmark was missing. Silent and red-faced, I finally dropped the Concordance to the floor and continued the sermon from memory.

After worship, I followed Ray's pickup truck home. His wife and two children went into the house and Ray showed me the tractors and harvester in his barn.

Later, around the table after grace, we were passing food around to fill our plates when Ray's youngest child, a seventeen-year-old girl, said to me, "I thought that big book was the Bible."

"It sure made a big bang when it hit the floor," her older sister said.

My face flushed again.

"Mr. Wood, I don't know what you were going to read from that book," said Mary, Ray's wife, "but I thought your message was just fine without it. You see, we like to hear what the preacher thinks about the Bible story, not what some person we hardly know has to say about it."

"We can read," Ray said, "but during worship, we are hoping to hear what the Holy Spirit is going to say through the man who is preaching."

"It's sort of like getting milk from your own cow instead of going to the store in town and getting it from some strange cow," his wife said.

Driving back to Oberlin, I thought about Ray and Mary's wisdom: their teaching that parishioners prefer spiritual food from someone who knows them and speaks from their heart. I tried to imagine their needs, their concern for a good harvest, the sick and housebound among them. I felt myself caring about them.

In succeeding weeks, I thought about scripture with the community I would visit in mind: the parables of Jesus and episodes of healing, for instance. I looked for rural life sermon illustrations. Comfort, coping, faith, and hope became major sermon themes. I began to preach from an outline instead of a prepared text and tried to speak from my heart. Parishioners responded by saying, "Good sermon, preacher," or "that sermon really spoke to me this morning."

Back on campus, over meals in the refectory or bull sessions in the evening, my classmates and I compared our field placement experiences. We debated immortality, the Trinity, miracles, and sin. We discussed what we knew about foreign missions, the Dead Sea Scrolls, church music, or social action. We compared lecture notes and studied for exams together. We seldom talked of personal matters. When anyone asked about girls, I told them about Helen.

"I had been engaged to be married," I said, "but my bride-to-be changed her mind."

I longed for a connection with a homosexual, and although I kept my eyes and ears open for signs, none came.

At the end of the year, I felt I had learned a lot from both books and people.

When I pulled into our driveway back in Bomoseen, I saw my father cultivating his garden and almost wept for joy. I beeped my horn. He looked up, grinned, and dropped his hoe, as Mother came out the back door. I hugged her, and my father hugged me.

"Glad to have you home for the summer," he said.

"Let's help him get his car unpacked," Mother said.

When he was out of earshot, Mother whispered, "He's driving again, but he is still smoking. Doctors have told me that he might have lapses in his mental state every seven years for the rest of his life."

That summer, I worked as a camp counselor during the week. Mother, Father, and I went to the movies on Saturday nights, and attended church on Sunday. My father said grace at our meals, and he talked about current events and injected humor into our conversations. Mother cooked and cleaned as she always had. She seemed happier, lighter. My brother, his wife, and their young son came for several visits. Our family felt whole again, and I was feeling much less anxious on my drive to Oberlin to begin my second year.

A Split Life

> Who am I? This or the Other? Am I one person today, and tomorrow another? Am I both at once? A hypocrite before others, and before myself, a contemptible woebegone weakling? Who am I? They mock me, these lonely questions of mine. Whoever I am, Thou knowest, O God, I am thine!
>
> —Dietrich Bonhoeffer, *The Cost of Discipleship*

During the first few months of my middler year, I read a newspaper article describing Kinsey's book about male sexuality. I found a copy of the book in the campus bookstore. Kinsey's projections shocked me. He was claiming that four percent of adult males were exclusively homosexual, thirteen percent incidentally homosexual, and thirty-seven percent had homosexual experiences at some point in their lives. Until that time, I could have counted the number of homosexuals I encountered on two hands, and there didn't seem to be another one at Oberlin.

While reading Kinsey, I was taking another course taught by Dr. May, requiring students to reconstruct the life of an Old Testament character. I wrote about the friendship between Jonathan and David as described in 1 Samuel 20. I was particularly struck by the emotion shared between David and Jonathan in verse 41: "As soon as the boy had gone, David rose from beside the stone heap and prostrated himself with his face to the ground. He bowed three times, and they kissed each other and wept with each other; David wept the more."

To my historical reconstruction of the beginning of the monarchy in Israel, I added my opinion that David and Jonathan might have been engaged in a homosexual relationship. I expected a bad grade, but May wrote, "Both men later married and became fathers but who knows what teenagers do when they get together?"

That same semester Horton assigned students to use theology to help a friend with a problem. I wrote a fictional dialog about a boy who spoke to his pastor because he was confused about how to reconcile his faith with his sexuality:

"Look, I don't expect you to understand, but I'm a homosexual," the boy said. "I know it's wrong, but I have the urges, and I've acted on them."

"Have you sought help for this problem?" the pastor asked.

"I tried to talk with my pastor, but he seemed uncomfortable," the boy said. "He didn't have any books to recommend and told me that it was a phase I was going through, that it would pass. Sometimes I think I have this affliction because I'm being punished for something."

"I'm afraid I don't know much about the subject," the pastor said. "But this I do know. Jesus still loves you. God knows what is happening to you. You need to pray about this. Your homosexuality is not a punishment. You are just trying to work out your personal life. God will help."

Horton wrote on the cover page: "Your friend is obviously not a Christian, and the pastor should have done more to help him become one."

I didn't argue. I was afraid Horton would think I was a homosexual: I had not forgotten about Igler. By introducing the subject of homosexuality, I felt myself flirting with disaster. I thought, if I didn't push the subject, the subject wouldn't harm me. I wouldn't mention it again, not even to students.

As I had done in Pennsylvania and Lake Placid, I began to take walks, hoping for some kind of eye contact or gesture that would reveal a mutual understanding or connection. Often, I walked to the undergraduate library, with the excuse of reading periodicals unavailable in the seminary library.

One night, while reading *The Saturday Review of Literature*, I noticed a student staring at me. He stood and smiled. I smiled back, and he pulled up a chair beside me.

"I've not seen you here before," he said.

"I'm from the Seminary."

"Oh."

"And you?"

"The Conservatory of Music, a piano major."

He was too young to be a veteran, but handsome, pleasant, and very self-confident.

"Would you care to see my little room?" he asked.

"Sure," I said.

"My roommates will not know what to do with a seminary student," he said, smiling.

"Roommates?" I asked.

"Yeah. There are three of us, and we have the largest room in the undergraduate dorm. We call it the Throne Room."

As we walked across campus, he talked about music theory, practice, senior recitals, and moving to New Jersey when he graduated. I told him about seminary life.

"No one knows me there," I said. "I can't take any chances."

"Your secret will be safe with us," he said. I had heard that before.

"I'd like for you to meet my friend, Bob, from the School of Theology," Jack said as we entered his room.

"Oh, my God, it's Mother Mary, confession time," said one of his roommates, in a high, lilting voice, his arms gesturing grandly.

The Throne Room was twice the size of my dorm room. Three beds with large cushions lined three walls. Drapes of fabric matching the cushions covered the windows. Burning incense filled the room with a sweet smell. Fresh flowers and framed photos of movie stars and musicians decorated desks.

"And who are you?" I asked the expressive one.

"I'm Jacqueline," he said.

"That's Billy Joe," Jack said. "His daddy happens to be a Southern Baptist preacher and he loves to save souls, but I'm afraid I'm going to burn in hell despite all his best efforts."

"That's why he lights the incense all the time. He's gettin' used to the flame," said Jack's other roommate.

"I'm Jasmine," he said. "Please to make your acquaintance."

He held out a limp hand attached to a long arm. I think he wanted me to kiss it. I felt myself tense up.

"Oh, relax," he said. "We're not going to bite you."

"That's Peter," Jack said.

I asked Peter about his major.

"Music, music, music. Can't you tell?"

"Well, Jasmine darling, you were almost a history major last night?" Jacqueline said.

"His history professor stopped by for a visit," Jack said.

"I think he really likes me," Jasmine said, "at least that's what he said."

"He told me the same thing last week, dearie," Jacqueline quipped.

"Who can we believe around here?" Jack said, laughing.

"Will it offend your friend if we shed a few of our rags?" Jasmine asked.

"I've seen your nude body," Jack said, "and you look better with your rags on."

"Why, you little bitch," Jasmine said.

Just then there was a rap at the door.

"Did anyone order a pizza?" Jack asked.

"I ordered the pizza man," Jacqueline said.

"I have to go," I said, feeling nervous.

"I hope it was not something I said?" Jasmine said.

"Not that I know of," I said.

"Well then, do come when you can stay longer. You can find a bride here," Jacqueline said.

"And what do you think your daddy would say if you came home with a preacher?" asked Jack.

"Why, he'd faint."

"I'll see ya," I said to Jack.

I didn't feel comfortable with this group. Nothing seemed serious to them. Everything was light and laughter. I returned to the seminary campus, thinking I would avoid the Throne Room in the future. Looking back, I confess that such negative feelings were evidence of internalized homophobia, as it would come to be called decades later. Military rules, "Q"'s in stockades, the Igler affair, the Scriptures condemning homosexuality, my childhood and parents' expectations for me to marry a woman encouraged this closet life, as it would be called. At the end of my second year in seminary, my secret was still safe.

Realizing that the summer of 1950 would be my last summer before beginning work in some capacity, I decided to forego my job as camp counselor and take a vacation. I knew one person in Manhattan, Margaret "Dee" Delano, who worked for *Reader's Digest*. Dee's parents were friends of my parents. I wrote Dee, hoping she would invite me to New York, and she did, for the July 4 weekend.

Dee rented a cottage on Fire Island for the summer with several of her girlfriends. One of Dee's friends, Carol, invited her cousin, Roger, an aspiring writer from Oklahoma.

The girls' bedrooms were on the second floor. Roger and I shared the attic.

Dee suggested we walk to Cherry Grove, "where all the homosexuals hang out. I know a good restaurant there, and we'll protect you," she said to Roger and me, laughing. Along the beach, handsome men in skimpy bathing suits sunned. I wanted to look but I didn't want to appear obvious. When we reached the restaurant, I had to go to the bathroom, where I discovered walls covered with invitations for sex, complete with graphic art.

A waiter came to our table and said, "I would like to welcome these two handsome men to Cherry Grove."

The girls quickly said, "They're with us."

"What a shame," the waiter replied.

That night Roger and I were changing out of our bathing suits when Roger asked what I thought about the restaurant.

"Did you see the graffiti?" he asked.

Instantly, we knew. We kissed, giggled, and joked about how the girls hadn't protected us enough. Roger was short, muscular, with broad shoulders, and wore boots and jeans. I liked his deep voice and masculinity.

On Sunday the girls returned to Manhattan for work. Roger and I volunteered to stay at the house to clean, shop for groceries, and have everything ready for the following weekend. As soon as the ferry departed, we raced back to the house, made love, and headed for Cherry Grove.

That week, we walked to Cherry Grove, swam, and talked about each other's ambitions to become journalists. Roger had a job lined up as a scriptwriter for a new radio show, "The Cliché Club" hosted by Bennett Cerff.

The following week, we took a furnished apartment on St. Luke's Place in Greenwich Village, and through the New York City Council of Churches I found work as a youth director for a black church in Brooklyn.

After work, Roger and I explored Times Square together. We strolled through Washington Square and Greenwich Village, in and out of art galleries, shops, and many gay bars. We even held hands in public. I felt extremely happy, thinking that Roger would be the one with whom I would share my life. We had been together for five weeks when, handing me his share of the apartment rent, Roger told me he had met someone else who had asked him to move in with him.

At work that day I hoped Roger's words about leaving had been a bad dream. But when I returned home, I discovered he had moved out. Tearfully, I cleaned our apartment, arranged for the phone to be disconnected, and negotiated the final rent payments with the landlord. The last time I saw Roger, he was eating lunch with his new friend under the great statue of Prometheus in Rockefeller Center.

Ordained

On June 17, 1951, the Ecclesiastical Council of the Rutland Association of Congregational Christian Churches convened at my home church, the First Congregational Church of Fair Haven, Vermont. The Council—forty-six lay and clergy people from churches throughout the association—had assembled to examine my fitness for ordination. Prior to the meeting, council members received and presumably read my ordination paper.

Waiting for the meeting to begin, I sat on the front pew, staring at a white Vermont marble baptismal font beside the chancel. Sacraments came to mind. Baptism and communion,

I rehearsed quietly to myself, are the outward and visible signs of inward and spiritual grace. Believers are baptized once, but communion is available every month, a reminder to see, touch and taste through symbols the body and blood of Jesus, to be reminded of the Last Supper when Jesus encouraged his disciples to love one another. I hoped my words would flow quickly, naturally. I thought about infant baptism. Parents bring their baby to be baptized to express their commitment to raise their child in a Christian home. Parishioners witnessing the baptism, through an implied covenant, agree to help the parents fulfill that commitment.

"I hope they don't ask me about my plans for marriage," I thought. "God help me to have the right words."

Behind me sat Dr. Herbert May, my parents, and the Council members, several of whom I had known before I went to college.

The Moderator, a former classmate from Oberlin, stood before the assembly, prayed, then said, "Bob, would you please read your ordination paper?"

I read it. Questions followed.

An older woman from a seat near the back of the church stood.

"Mr. Wood, what are your thoughts about the Bible?" she asked.

"My study of the Bible, though extensive, is incomplete," I said. "I do not know what parts are absolutely true, what passages are open to broader interpretation, or what phrases might be added and for what purposes. Not every word is equal to every other word, for surely the 'begats' are not as important as the dying words of Jesus. But within and among its words are to be found the answers to life, love, and hope. I know that interpreting the Bible requires discipline and study. Until another prophet of God walks the earth, and we can record his deeds and words, the Bible must remain in its state, perfect and imperfect, as the basis of Christian religion."

"Is the Bible the inspired Word of God?" she asked.

"Yes," I answered. "The Bible is certainly written by human beings, but I look on the words of the Bible as having been inspired by each author's belief in God. I also believe that God used the writers to convey a spiritual message, particularly through what is written about the nature of God and the life, death, and resurrection of Jesus."

"Speaking of Jesus," one of the pastors on the Council said, "what do you believe about Jesus?"

"Jesus was a living example of the ability and design of God. Christ appeared long enough to sow the seed and should be worshiped as an intermediary, not as the original. Jesus is not coequal with God: He is the Son of God. He exemplified the Christian way of giving, not only money and time, but of body, mind, and soul as well. Christ, as our example, gave himself completely to God."

"Do you believe in prayer?" a woman asked.

"Yes, I'm praying now."

Laughter erupted. I saw the humor, smiled, and waited for quiet to return.

"I pray because I cannot live unaided. I pray because I know my prayers are heard and answered by some force more powerful than any in the world. I truly believe that I am alive today because of prayer. I also offer up simple prayers of thanks and petition because I can conceive of no mortal being responsible for the outcome of various actions. I need no other person to assist me in my prayers or to carry my petitions to Almighty God. I pray each day, tendering new requests for aid in meeting today's problems. My prayers can transcend time and space and person, and I know they bring results."

"What can you tell us about your military service?" was the next question.

I told them the story.

"Why do you want to be ordained?" another minister asked.

"It is my one desire to serve God. I cannot live a contented life in the years ahead if I do nothing to be of service to the people of this world. My person is nothing but how I can be used to help bring the Kingdom of God on earth and is limited only by the powers of God. I am ignorant and sinful, desiring only to use myself that more people might come to know God as a friend and father."

"Why did you choose Oberlin?"

"I lived in Lorain as a child and had remembered being on campus. It was affiliated with the Congregational Church and had a fine reputation for training pastors."

An elderly man stood up and asked, "It also has a reputation for being liberal. Do you believe that morals are relative or absolute?"

This one was a trap, I thought.

"Morals are relative. In my experience, there are exceptions to everything. Absolute standards exclude. When morals are perceived as absolute, we become judgmental. In my opinion, judgment is God's work. Matthew 7:1 reads, 'Judge not, that you be not judged.'"

My answer didn't seem to impress the man who had asked the question. A murmur sounded in the congregation, as if perhaps I had said something wrong.

Another older man, bald and bent over, stood up.

"There's nothing in that young man's paper I couldn't agree with one hundred percent," he said.

"Are we ready to vote?" asked the moderator.

I was escorted to an adjoining room. The Ecclesiastical Council voted, then adjourned to eat.

That evening, almost forty people—my parents, family, area pastors and church members filed back into the pews. I wore a new robe my parents had given me for graduation.

For a prelude, the organist played Gounod's "Sanctus" from *St. Cecelia Mass*, followed by the hymn, "Holy, Holy, Holy." Rev. George Brown, pastor of host church, offered the call to worship and invocation. Rev. Olaf Johnson read Isaiah 61:1: "'The spirit of the Lord God is upon me because the Lord has anointed me; he has sent me to bring good news to the oppressed, to bind up the brokenhearted, to proclaim liberty to the captives and release to the prisoners.'"

"Yes, that is exactly what I want to do," I thought.

May preached about how important the discovery of the Dead Sea Scrolls had been. Although the Isaiah scroll was carbon dated to the time of Jesus, May couldn't prove that Jesus read from that specific scroll. Yet, May preached, "The message would have been clear if Jesus had read it. Jesus would have seen Isaiah's warning that prophets could expect rejection and exile, and that faith in God, alone, would allow them, despite the consequences, to accomplish God's work on earth. And Isaiah's only reward, the only reward you can expect Bob, was to fulfill his calling."

That I had anything in common with Isaiah was an awe-inspiring thought. I felt myself, through May's words, connected, joined, to all who had been and presently were called into God's service. Singing the hymn, "Forward Through the Ages," encouraged my thinking of Christian history as filled with remarkable stories of calling. After the hymn Rev. Helen Lyman, pastor of the United Church in Benson, Vermont, announced that the vote of the Ecclesiastical Council to grant me ordination was unanimous.

Rev. Graydon Brown invited all ordained ministers to the chancel. Twenty came, old and young, men and women. They surrounded me. "Robert, would you please kneel for the laying on of hands?" Brown asked. I knelt before them. He instructed the ministers to put their hands on my head and join him in prayer. He prayed. I do not remember his prayer, but I remember the feeling of being supported and of God's presence. I felt peace and exhilaration and imagined the scene in which John the Baptist baptized Jesus when the dove was sent from heaven to land on Jesus' head. I wept in joy. I remained full of emotion as the conference minister prayed and the moderator welcomed me to Christian ministry.

Finding Work

In October 1951, I moved into a furnished room at the University of Pennsylvania Club on West Fifty-Sixth Street, a short walk from Carnegie Hall and Central Park. Most Club residents were older businessmen who resided in the city during the week. Dressed in suits and ties, these men left early for work and returned at day's end, often stopping in the bar for a drink before going to their rooms. A few, like me, were young college graduates beginning their careers.

Finding work in a church was going to take time. Meanwhile, I had the day-to-day expenses of living in New York. I mailed resumes in response to ads I read in the newspaper and landed a job at United World Films, writing study booklets, advertising copy, and promotional letters about religious films. When club residents asked how my new job was going, I told them it paid the bills. But barely. The job paid ninety-seven dollars a week, hardly enough money to cover my expenses at the Club.

Many of my new neighbors settled into a routine of eating dinner in the Club dining room, then smoking a cigar in the library where they sat in leather-bound chairs, watching a black-and-white television set. One night, I peeked in the library door to see how much smoke was hanging in the air. Too much smoke affected my breathing, traces of the lung infections from my war wound.

"Come on in, Bob," one of the younger residents said. I entered and sat beside him in the back of the room.

"What's on television?"

"Democracy at work," he replied. "Senator Joseph McCarthy interrogating a man from Hollywood."

I watched McCarthy interrogate others, attacking some as full-fledged communists, others as communist sympathizers. "Pinkos" he called them. I also heard his claims that homosexuals were a national-security risk. Federal employees suspected of being homosexual should be fired, according to McCarthy. "Homo-perverts," he called them.

"Somebody has to defend truth and democracy," the young man beside me said. I didn't reply.

McCarthy frightened me. I had read a recent issue of *Pastoral Psychology* about the work of George W. Henry, an associate professor of clinical psychiatry at Cornell University. Henry warned of a growing public resentment towards homosexuals. Because of McCarthy, courts were issuing harsher prison sentences for convicted homosexuals. Instead of such sentences, Henry advised that homosexuals should receive therapy for their "deep-rooted personality disorder." I hadn't thought about myself in those terms. The summer before, I had enjoyed socializing in the gay bars in Greenwich Village. They had been fun, relaxed places to meet men. Now stories of McCarthy, police raids, muggings, and blackmail made me afraid of going to bars. I stored the few sex books I owned in a Cole metal file case to conceal them from the maid who made the beds each day.

That night, through the only window in my room, I stared out on a courtyard surrounded by tall buildings. Looking out upon the empty space between the buildings, I felt alone and confused. I imagined people living behind adjacent windows, perhaps the same people I saw crowding busy sidewalks during the day.

"God, you know my heart," I prayed. "You know my soul. You know the dreams that I dream and the physical attractions I feel. You know if they are bad or good. You know if I am sick or evil. You know if I am a pervert. Heal me Lord, if I am sick. Forgive me, Lord, if I am evil. Guide me. Protect me. I give myself to you. In Jesus's name, Amen."

The prayer did not take the lingering moral and psychological confusion about my homosexuality away, nor did it take away my fantasies or desire to be intimate with a man.

The following day, out of habit, I attended the Broadway Tabernacle, a Congregational church just a short walk from where I lived. Fine choral music echoed in the cathedral like space. Exquisite woodcarvings and stained glass added to an ambiance of mystery.

Rev. Dr. Albert Penner, the senior pastor there, preached about the growing casualties of war in the Korean conflict, and proposed that our country was not coming together as it did during the Second World War.

"Freedom and democracy," he said, "are obtained through sacrifice. And those young boys who are fighting on the front lines deserve and need our prayers."

I was moved by his sermon, so in subsequent weeks I returned to hear him preach. Penner deftly handled the interpretation of scripture. He reminded me of the needs of others and challenged me to expect more out of life for myself.

In January, through the Cory Book Service, I discovered *The Homosexual in America* by Donald Webster Cory. I couldn't put the book down. Page after page, Cory described homosexual culture in ways that were familiar to me. There was a chapter on the various types of homosexuals, from those who tended to be effeminate and girly to those who tended to be muscular and manly. Other chapters described cruising in parks and movie houses and types of couples. He wrote about prejudice—homosexuals unfairly treated by employers, family members, and landlords. His descriptions of laws prohibiting homosexual activity, police entrapment, and court-ordered lobotomies shocked and further frightened me. His nonjudgmental speculations about the causes of homosexuality and the futility of treatments and cures made sense to me. He even included a chapter addressed to parents encouraging them to love and support their homosexual sons or daughters. In his book, Cory excluded any concern about church or spirituality.

When I finished the book, I wanted to meet Cory, talk to him, so I wrote him a letter. To my surprise, Cory wrote back that he would be pleased to meet me and included his telephone number. I called and we set a time to meet.

Cory was a nervous-looking, thin man, a bit shorter than me. He wore casual clothes. He introduced himself as Ed Sagarin and talked about his job as an olfactory researcher for a cosmetics company. He feared losing his job. He had written his book, "to put flesh and blood on Kinsey's statistics."

"The editors were reluctant to use the word homosexual in the title," he said. "They were afraid of being labeled a homosexual press. But I wanted those who purchased the book and librarians to have to say the word. That was the only way to get the subject out in front of the American public."

Cory listened as I told him about Scott, Jimmy, Rittenhouse Square, the Throne Room, and Roger. I told him that fidelity was important to me and about my dream of finding a man with whom I could share my life.

"Good luck," he said, and warned that homosexuals tended to be promiscuous.

I explained my desire to serve God in a local church.

"You're going to need a miracle," he replied.

"Why did you write so little about faith and religion in your book?" I asked.

"I don't know much about religion," he said. "If you're so interested in religion, why don't you write a book? You're the ordained minister."

He asked if I was able to make any friends in Manhattan, and I told him about my fear of going to the bars.

"You might be interested in joining a group that meets in my apartment," he said. "It's not church but you're welcome to come."

The following week, I took a subway to Greenwich Village. Sagarin had drawn the curtains in his apartment. Fifteen casually dressed men, ages twenty-five to forty, sat on cushions in his living room. We introduced ourselves, first names only. I identified myself as Rev. Bob. A man calling himself Dave talked about a sister who "knew" and yet was supportive. Charles talked about his landlady's threats to evict him. Bill, an actor, described an older producer who expected sex from him.

Sagarin listened and kept the group focused. I felt a lot of pain in the room, from people like me trying to cope. Toward the end of the meeting, a man described that Mattachine—a West Coast activist group—was starting a chapter in Manhattan. He gave the meeting time and date.

Mattachine met in a private apartment. The word *Mattachine*, I learned, was another word for court jester—a professional entertainer and/or prophet for Italian nobility. In medieval days, the court jester was considered a man of wisdom, the only one who could speak truth to the king without being penalized. Court jesters faced grave consequences when their predictions were wrong. Mattachine organizers described plans to speak truth concerning gay rights. Rights? I thought to myself. I had been thinking about homosexuality as a crime or a psychological illness. The idea of homosexual rights never occurred to me.

They shared testimonies about the negative consequences of being homosexual. I listened as men told stories of being disowned by parents, imprisonment, and loneliness. My memories of these stories haunted me during Sunday morning worship at the Broadway Tabernacle. As Penner preached about and prayed for the disadvantaged and downtrodden, I projected into his words my concern for the men whose needs had been made known to me. As I looked around the congregation, I noticed other single men, alone, and wondered about their needs.

Rev. Joe Huntley, Penner's associate at Broadway Tabernacle, was a short, stocky, round-faced man, with thick brown hair who dressed in stylish suits and ties. Huntley seemed infinitely more settled and self-assured than I did even though we were about the same age. Seeing him, robed and assisting Penner, caused me to revel in thoughts about my own future as a pastor. I could see myself standing in robes before a congregation, preaching and praying.

During church announcements, Huntley frequently invited single men and women of the parish to join him for Sunday brunch. One Sunday in February 1952, feeling a need to make friends beyond the gatherings at Sagarin's and Mattachine, I joined Huntley and a small group of younger parishioners at the Essex House, which overlooked Central Park South. Huntley came alone, so I assumed he was single.

As we ate, he led a discussion about Penner's sermon. Afterwards, he asked us how we came to be in New York and about our personal ambitions. Huntley had a way of relating a statement of interest spoken by a member of our group to the programmatic opportunities at Broadway Tabernacle. Feeling shy, I didn't contribute to the conversation.

Huntley drew me out the following week.

"What brings you to New York?" he asked.

I told my story of calling, academic preparation, and ordination into Christian ministry.

Afterwards, Huntley invited me to his apartment, nearby. Outside the Essex House, Huntley lit a fat cigar, and we walked fast in the February cold.

"How long have you been attending Broadway Tabernacle?" he asked.

"About six months. Long enough to be thinking about becoming a member. And you? How long have you been here?"

"Three years next month," he said. "I served two years in Detroit before coming here."

"What a great church to continue your ministry."

"Yes. I can't imagine a better church. What's keeping you from serving a church?"

"I had to take a job in order to cover my expenses here."

I was describing my job selling films as we arrived at Huntley's apartment building. We took an elevator to the fourth floor. Huntley offered a quick tour of his bedroom, a second, smaller bedroom he used as a study, and a triangular, walk-through kitchen. We sat in his living room.

"Where did you go to seminary?" I asked.

"Heidelberg. I was ordained in the Evangelical and Reformed Church tradition. You must be aware that leaders of the Evangelical and Reformed Churches and Congregational Christian Churches have begun talks about a merger. The merger is years away but I'm glad to be living in an age where denominations are exploring their common ground. But enough church talk. Do you have a girlfriend?"

"I don't date women," I said.

"Then how do you spend your free time?"

"I've attended a few Mattachine meetings," I said.

I felt Mattachine was like a code word. If Huntley knew about it, he would know I made a personal revelation about myself without having said the actual word. If he made the connection and disliked homosexuals, he could ask me to leave. I feared he would.

"May I go with you to the next meeting?" Huntley asked after a smile. "It would be an opportunity for us to be with our own kind, wouldn't it?"

Hearing these words caused a slight euphoria within me. I couldn't believe it.

"Does Penner know?"

"Know what?"

"Know about you?"

"We haven't discussed it. He hasn't asked. It's really nobody's business. So, are you looking for church work?"

"Yes."

"You'll want to make an appointment with Donald Strickler. He's the Conference Minister of the Metropolitan Association. You can be open with him. I was. He knows about confidentiality."

"Are you sure?"

"Trust me."

"I never dreamed that you were a, like me?"

"How would you?" he interrupted. "Unless I told you. But Bob, I don't talk about it."

"Don't worry. I won't say a word."

I left Huntley's apartment feeling a small miracle had just taken place. Before meeting Huntley, I doubted I would find placement within a church, despite my belief in God and ordination. Now, I saw possibilities. If Huntley was serving a church, I could too.

Two weeks later, Strickler invited me to lunch at a restaurant near Gramercy Park. Photographs of celebrities who had previously dined there lined the walls. The waiters, all men, knew their regular customers by name. Strickler, it seemed to me, was a regular. After our meal and a cordial conversation, he handed me a three-page form to fill out, a ministerial profile.

"Be sure to include the fact that you are a veteran," Strickler said several times. "And list any organizations to which you belong."

"I belong to Mattachine," I said, trying out the code word again.

"What's Mattachine?" he asked.

I explained.

"Well, you don't have to tell them everything. On my first profile, I didn't tell them that I voted for FDR," he said.

I followed his advice and wrote about my Christian upbringing, college, combat service, and seminary. I described my style of preaching as "Biblically based"—meaning I used the Bible as my point of departure for sermons—and listed my experiences in Christian Education and camp counseling, including my job in Brooklyn. I concluded with a statement of faith lifted from my ordination paper.

Strickler read my profile and approved. He would circulate copies to Metropolitan Area churches searching for leadership and promised his personal recommendation.

"Bob, you have an advocate within the denomination, but you must be discreet," he said. "You don't want to tell too much about yourself."

I could make such an accommodation, I thought, if it meant getting a church position.

A month later, Huntley offered me a part-time job managing a USO for the Armed Services on Friday evenings, organizing social events for young people on Saturday evenings, and conducting tours of the church on Sunday afternoons.

Broadway Tabernacle's pulpit was prestigious. When Penner was away, guest preachers came from as far away as England. Huntley substituted when conflicts in scheduling arose. On Labor Day Sunday in 1953, Penner was away, Huntley was unavailable, and no guest preachers were scheduled. The job of preaching fell to me.

I felt exhilarated and intimidated as I mounted the eagle pulpit to preach a sermon based on Luke 6:27–36. My sermon, entitled "Being Good Is Not Enough," exhorted listeners to consider Christ's teaching about love related to personal income and human need, and to fight selfishness by spending in sacrificial ways to help those less fortunate.

After the service a group of parishioners approached me. I assumed they wanted a tour. About half the congregation on any given Sunday were tourists eager to know more about the building. I enjoyed pointing out the bullet hole in the Eagle pulpit attributed to a southerner who had objected to a sermon about abolition during the Civil War.

"We're from Rockland County," one of them said. "Donald Strickler told us that we could hear you preach, today. Is there a place in the church where we might sit and talk with you for a while?"

We met in a large oak-paneled lounge with a fireplace. Oil portraits of Broadway Tabernacle pastors dating back to pre-Civil War years were hung around the room. Members of the group introduced themselves by name, position of leadership within their church, and vocation. Among them were a grocery store owner, a research scientist, a grade school principal, a bookkeeper, and several housewives. All had read my ministerial profile.

"We serve the Search Committee at the First Congregational Church in Spring Valley, New York," said Keith Apgar. "That's in Rockland County, near Nyack where the newly constructed Tappan Zee Bridge comes across the Hudson from Westchester. We've read your profile. I think we were all impressed by your service in the Second World War as well as your church background within the Congregational denomination. But we note your lack of hands-on experience ministering to and leading a local congregation."

"My experience consists only of field work in seminary and my work here at Broadway," I said. "If I were to become your pastor, I expect I would be learning and growing in my skills while I sought to bring the Gospel message and the spirit of the living Christ to you and your families and to your community."

"We feel our church needs long-range leadership," Apgar said. "How long would you expect to remain in your first parish?"

"At least ten years: time to get acquainted, time to assess needs, time to chart a future, and time to implement goals. In other words, time for planting seeds and time to harvest."

"That sounds reasonable," one of the ladies said.

Another committee member described anticipated population growth in Spring Valley, citing the new bridge and cheaper real estate prices on their side of the Hudson.

"We want a young, aggressive minister to build up the congregation," he said.

"I could work at that."

"Do you do your own cooking?" another lady asked. "I ask because I note that you are single."

"My mother taught me how to shop, cook, and do the laundry."

"Good for her," the lady said.

"Tell us about your tour of duty," Keith asked. I think my stories of war impressed them more than my theology. After forty-five minutes of questions and answers, they invited me to preach at their church.

Parishioners must have been pleased with the sermon because they voted unanimously to call me to be their pastor. In December 1953, I moved to Spring Valley.

Ministry

Spring Valley's squared city blocks, with single-family houses and manicured lawns reminded me of my hometown of Youngstown, Ohio. The church's white clapboard exterior resembled my home church in Vermont. The parsonage had a living room, formal dining room, three bedrooms, two baths, a full attic, and basement. Having occupied a furnished room, I couldn't furnish such a house in the beginning, so I moved into a renovated second floor apartment owned by one of the parishioners.

Through my planning for worship each Sunday, I sought to guide the congregation in their thinking about God and the church. I planned my sermons well in advance and tried to vary the scripture texts and subjects. For inspiration, I relied on the church calendar, read newspapers every day, listened to parishioners, and kept abreast of the changes taking place in our denomination related to the merger. Church rolls listed 140 members, but only seventy or so attended on an average Sunday. If we were lucky, we hit 100 on holy days.

That first year of ministry, I also dedicated myself to becoming acquainted with all the parishioners. I made 547 pastoral calls in parishioners' homes, at hospitals, a tuberculosis sanatorium, and the county jail. As I had been taught in seminary, I made eleven home visits a week. On 3" x 5" cards, I noted names addresses, telephone numbers, and directions. I also jotted down personal information such as "shut-in," "recovering from surgery," "widow," "small children," "cool house," "good cook," "lonely," "hard of hearing," "a little feeble," "likes Scripture read," or "likes a prayer." I made note of their friends and relatives active in the church. Often, I would break the ice by asking people how they came to be associated with the church. Most shared readily their personal histories, problems, joys, beliefs, thoughts about former pastors, and opinions about controversies.

A dedicated few ran the church. They attended church, almost without fail. Some sang in the choir. Others ushered and helped with the offering. They provided financial support and served on boards and committees, where they made decisions about programs, building maintenance, and budgets. Through their leadership, church members voted to begin a $40,000 building expansion. To raise money, the trustees voted to rent the parsonage.

All was going well until prejudice reared its ugly head when the trustees voted to rent to a Black couple.

Peter Murdock, a real estate agent, began a campaign expressing an opinion that the trustees made a mistake renting to Blacks. I made an appointment to visit him. One of the trustees warned that he could be outspoken.

"Be diplomatic, but don't give in to him," he said.

His large house sat on a hill, and he was waiting outside when I drove up. He was short and broad-shouldered, a bulldog kind of man.

As we walked around his garden, he talked about hybrids, feeding, watering, and beetles. He called each rose by name. I was sniffing a fragrant rose when he spoke.

"Bylaws don't permit you to vote on the trustees, but you were there, and they probably sought your opinion," he said. "I assume you wanted those niggers to move into the parsonage."

I was stunned to hear that slanderous word coming from a parishioner.

"The trustees rented to them because they were the first couple to answer the ad."

"You know that my business is real estate and I'm here to tell you that if you let them stay, we're going to lose money. It's proven that once they move into a neighborhood, the real estate values go down. You'd better listen to me. I know what I'm talking about."

"I'm sure you do, Peter, but the bylaws give the trustees authority to manage the properties of our church. They've exercised this authority, and I stand behind them."

"You're going to regret it because I'm not going to stand by and let our church get a reputation to being insensitive to our neighbors."

I could see that he would not be moved in his thinking.

The following Sunday, hoping to inspire confidence in the trustees' decision, I preached a sermon on tolerance.

"We tolerate others," I preached, "so that others will tolerate us."

I quoted the Old Testament prophets who encouraged the faithful to do justice and love mercy. I referred to the civil rights marches in Selma, Alabama.

"Tolerance is not giving in to prejudice but taking a position for the oppressed," I said.

A few months later, Murdock attended our annual meeting. His concerns were on the agenda. He made a motion that the trustees give the current tenants of the parsonage one month to vacate. People supporting Murdock spoke. Others argued to defend the trustees' decision. His motion prevailed by a simple majority of raised hands. A church vote, I realized, was how ill-contented parishioners exercised their power. My personal spiritual values of love and tolerance seemed at odds with the majority.

There were other minor controversies. Whatever the tension or conflict, I tried to minister to everyone, even those with whom I disagreed. Most seemed pleased by my ministry. Often, I felt God's hand on my shoulder and the Holy Spirit in my soul, infusing my heart with the love for these people who had called me to be their leader.

My life in Spring Valley, like the colors in the church chancel, remained organized around the holy seasons—Lent, Easter, Ascension, Pentecost, Thanksgiving, Advent, Christmas, Epiphany, Ash Wednesday, and Sunday worship. I found Communion particularly meaningful—our weak, sinful community of believers eating bread and drinking grape juice, joined symbolically in the suffering of Christ, moving towards the realization of the Kingdom of God.

Outside that community, I felt lonely, and gradually, imperceptibly, I began to feel the need for nurturing and love: I needed a friend or better yet, a lover. I was human: I had desire.

ADVOCACY

Mattachine conducted meetings at the Wendell Wilkie Memorial Building in Manhattan. I parked nearby, and stood across the street from the building, watching those entering the building. I thought I might spot police and FBI agents by the clothes they wore. We had been warned to do so.

Once I felt safe, I entered. The ground floor assembly hall held 100 or so portable chairs. Newsletters from Mattachine, the George Henry Foundation, One, Daughters of Bilitis, and other "homophile" groups were available on a table in the back of the room. I looked around the room for Dick Leitsch, the president of Mattachine. Dick arranged for and introduced speakers. He enlisted doctors, psychologists, social workers, and political activists to speak about problems homosexuals faced in society. Many of the speakers remained closeted, yet their speeches questioned long held notions of homosexuality as being a sickness, sin, or illegal. When Dick Leitsch discovered that I was a minister, he had asked me to speak. Feeling an obligation to minister to this community, I agreed, then prayed and prepared.

I read from the Bible, Psalm 88. The images offered by the psalmist of "a soul full of troubles," "forsaken among the dead," and "being cast off," seemed to mirror the testimonies I had heard from homosexuals describing their life circumstances. I described the stories of separation and isolation I heard. I spoke of those that had been shunned by friends, family members, and coworkers.

"Verse 9 of Psalm 88 offered a word of hope," I said. "'Every day I call upon Thee, O Lord; I spread out my hands to thee.'"

"In the midst of his despair, when it seemed all was lost, the psalmist prayed to God," I said. "Prayer is available to us as well unless we are cut off from God."

A barrage of questions followed.

"Why do you stay in a church that hates queers?"

"Why doesn't the church love us?"

"A friend of mine told me he couldn't receive the Sacrament if he had been in a gay bar the night before."

"I don't attend church anymore, nor do I give them any money. Maybe if they thought the way you do, but I don't see that any time soon. Do you?"

"I grew up in the church and I'm going to stay in the church, so I guess that means I'll always be in the closet. Do church officials know how you think?"

"What did the church do to help the boys of Boise?" one angry voice said, referring to the witch hunt of homosexuals in Boise, Idaho two years earlier, when in a city of forty thousand more than one thousand men had been questioned and nine had received fifteen-year prison terms.

I felt inadequate. I really didn't have answers. I took these voices of pain, anger, and betrayal into my heart, and prayed to find a way to minister to them. I sought out the few books about homosexuality and religion.

The British theologian D.S. Bailey's 1955 book *Homosexuality and the Western Christian Tradition* began by examining the Old Testament story of Sodom and Gomorrah. The sin that destroyed Sodom, Bailey concluded, was not sexual in nature, but rather a lapse in ancient Middle Eastern customs of hospitality. Bailey went on to show how Christian emperors, particularly Justinian, had used false interpretations of the Sodom story to justify laws against homosexuals, laws which had survived the Middle Ages to be codified in British law. Bailey argued for legal reform because, in his opinion, a genuine homosexual condition was morally neutral.

I used Bailey's position concerning the historical rejection of homosexuals by the church and began to describe ways in which homosexual love could be moral, then asked the question, "What response could homosexuals expect from the church, an institution organized around the principle of love?"

In January 1959, I presented a position paper to the Social Action Committee of the Metropolitan Association of Congregational Christian Churches. For several years, as one of my clerical responsibilities, I served on this committee that explored race, population and rent control, public safety, and economic justice issues. I stood before the committee as a pastor in their association, I learned in conversations before the meeting that several committee members assumed a ministry to homosexuals was unnecessary because there were no homosexuals in their churches.

I began my presentation with a quote from Ezekiel: "And I came to the exiles, and I sat there among them, stunned, for seven days." Then I explained the problem.

"It has always been the responsibility of the Church to broaden horizons, challenge the status quo when necessary, so the mores of God in Christ can more effectively be at work in the world," I said. "It is time the Church was called upon to use its channels of preaching, ministry, and education in meeting the problems, personal and social, engendered by the presence of homosexuality in our society."

I offered Kinsey's statistics to suggest the likelihood that a percentage of parishioners, whether confessed or not, were homosexuals. These church members, I added, are victims of prejudice, and deserve our ministry. I described homosexuals' experiences of dismissal from work, the burden of blackmail, and the usurpation of civil liberties, thinking about the men whose stories I had heard at Mattachine. I wrote about their loneliness and being forced to be hypocrites before family and friends.

I listed specific recommendations for beginning a ministry: publish articles in church publications, arrange for homosexual speakers at clergy retreat, create workshops on homosexuality in Associations and Conferences, network with other denominations, encourage local church studies and prayer cells. I also suggested a competent religious author might write a book about ministering to homosexuals. After considerable discussion, my paper was tabled, never to be brought up again by that committee.

I continued reading everything I could find on religion and homosexuality: a paragraph in one book, a historical footnote in another, a theological sentence or two tucked away in someone's treatise. I wrote in my spare time, without fear, because I doubted the work would ever be published. I reasoned that the writing, if nothing else, would help clarify my thinking on the subject.

Alone, I typed purposes for my work: to describe the many dimensions of homosexual life I was discovering, to encourage homosexuals not to abandon Christianity, and to exhort Church leaders and parishioners to express concern for homosexuals. Finally, I planned to state conditions under which homosexuality might be considered moral.

I began by creating fictionalized vignettes of homosexuals facing moral dilemmas that were based on actual stories I heard at Mattachine and in the bars.

About a lonely New York actor, I wrote, "It was one thing to feel alone out in a prairie town, but here in the heart of the Gay White Way it was all the more terrifying." I had been walking crowded streets, sitting in public parks, and squeezing into gay bars and parties, alone. I had personally felt this terrible loneliness.

About a public school teacher who joined a local church, I wrote, "He is a follower of Christ, but with the question: Can an overt homosexual be a Christian? These are not the guilt pangs of one who has just satisfied himself sexually, but the snapping of a conscience in a sensitive Christian who is walking a tightrope between the moral and immoral." I felt myself on a tightrope of sorts, not for my behavior, but for public reaction to my behavior.

To a soldier in Korea, I had a young man write: "As the snowflakes paint my brown glove an off-color white, and I blow them away, I blow them across the miles to you. For my kisses come on the tip of every snowflake to say how much my heart misses you and how anxious I am for your safety. Oh, my darling, take care, so next New Year's Eve we may both be here together." I imagined myself receiving such a letter and the profound romantic emotions felt by people who were in love but separated by miles.

I wrote about a father who affirmed his son's commitment to another man: "Well, instead of losing a son as most parents do, we gained one." I imagined how my own parents might react if I should bring home a lover with whom I wanted to share my life. I had no reason to believe that they would rejoice.

After the fictionalized vignettes, I shifted into the style of a thesis to portray homosexual culture beyond specific individuals. I wrote about the prevalence of homosexuals in fashion and public entertainment—set designers, choreographers, costumers, coiffures; about homosexual themes in movies such as *Advise and Consent*, *The Children's Hour*, *The Devil's Advocate*, *Victim*, *Rope*, *Compulsion*, *Suddenly Last Summer*, and *The Third Sex*; Broadway and Off Broadway productions such as *Cat on a Hot Tin Roof*, *Tea and Sympathy*, *The Third Person*, *Waiting for Godot*, and *Deathwatch*; and publications—photo magazines, novels, nonfiction, magazine advertisements, and greeting cards. To those who claimed not to know homosexuals, I wanted to show that they entertained us, dressed us, and served us in unseen ways every day.

I reiterated problems faced by homosexuals, according to Sagarin, and expanded the list to include issues that had surfaced in Mattachine: the threat of job loss, McCarthy's railings, blackmail, rejection at draft boards, dishonorable discharges, politically motivated clean ups, life in gay ghettos, fear, and negative psychology—being diagnosed as mentally ill, court-ordered lobotomies, and suicide. I wrote about the violation of civil liberties through unjust laws and police entrapment; the use of demeaning words like "fairies," "queers," "dykes," "pansies," "faggots," and "fruit"; and stereotypes of homosexuals as effeminate, promiscuous, seducers of minors. And as I wrote, I felt increased indignation toward the church and society.

When I wrote about the double life of homosexuals, I felt my own hypocrisy. Regretfully, I adopted the language of clinicians, describing homosexuality as an "affliction," a "problem," a "perversion," an "inner dilemma." Such language, I now recognize, protected me: I never proclaimed myself to be a homosexual, yet through my characters my feelings emerged.

However, I focused on how the church failed to reflect Christ in its response to homosexuals. I described the church as an oppressor, recalling Bailey's descriptions of Penitentials denying Communion to dying homosexuals and the practice of burying them alive; the seventeenth-century Lutheran professor who listed earthquakes, famine, and pestilence as results of homosexual vice; and Justinian's punishment of homosexuals: mutilation and castration, and dragging their limp bodies through the streets. I wept for those victims of hatred. I challenged biblical scholars to rethink Bible passages wrongly used to condemn homosexuality, and introduced scriptures which encouraged Christians to love their neighbors. I warned against passing judgment on others.

I wrote answers to the question: How would Jesus Christ have responded to homosexuals? "Jesus came to save the world, not to condemn it. His love, message, and life were given for all." To those about to stone the woman, Jesus said, "Let those without sin cast the first stone." He warned Pharisees not to be judgmental.

"Homosexuality is moral," I wrote, "because it presents an opportunity for love to those who are unable to find love in heterosexual relations. The most valid reason for wanting to marry is that two people love each other and wish to spend the rest of their lives in the closest possible relationship."

If called into Christian service, homosexuals could be ordained, I proclaimed.

Finally, I repeated the recommendations for the ministries previously stated in my position paper to the Social Action Committee and encouraged the establishment of an Institute on Christianity and Homosexuality.

I searched for a publisher, without success.

One day I saw an ad for Vantage Press in the *Herald Tribune*: "We will publish your book. Send manuscript for free evaluation." I wrote for information and received a pamphlet.

Vantage Press promised hardcover books with a dust jacket, promotion, and a national distribution, for a fee based on manuscript length.

Having described the subject of my proposed book, Vantage editors instructed me to mail the finished manuscript. Within two weeks after I had submitted it, I received an editor's opinion that my book merited publication. The cost: $3,500 for 5,000 books. Vantage required $1,000 up front, so I tapped my life insurance policy.

Christ and the Homosexual was published under my own name in 1960. John F. Kennedy was running for president against Richard Nixon. Stonewall was nine years away. The word *gay* was seldom used publicly, and the word *homophobia* had not been coined.

All 5,000 copies sold, I earned back my investment, and my message had a national audience. The book received two awards of merit and positive reviews in all the homophile publications published at the time, including *The Ladder*, published for and by lesbians.

I gave a copy of my book to my parents, who had sold their Vermont home and moved to Florida. Mother never talked about it. My father's first response was: "It certainly is an important subject, and the church should look at it." Later, Mother wrote that my father was upset by the book.

In a telephone conversation weeks later, my father made his final comment about the book.

"That section on sadomasochism bothered me," he said. "It was too descriptive, too pornographic. I wish you hadn't written that. I found it disturbing. I never thought a son of mine would write something like that."

His criticisms made me sad. He could not see good in what I had done.

My brother never commented on the book, nor did his wife who wrote letters peppered with tales of their growing children. They sent holiday cards and never missed a birthday, but not a word about my book.

I also gave copies of my book to members of the Church Council at Spring Valley. The only response from them I overheard in a conversation between two parishioners.

"Bob seems to know what he is talking about," was all that was said, but no one talked to me directly about it.

There were some complaints in letters I received. Some felt there was not enough detail about discrimination. Others were concerned that I hadn't mentioned famous homosexuals. Some felt I was too easy on church leaders, too East Coast oriented, and too religious or academic. I answered every letter sent with a return address.

Hundreds of letters arrived from Protestant ministers, Roman Catholic priests, college professors, social workers, psychologists, journalists, doctors, and many gay and lesbian readers. Many praised the book. Some requested more information. Others unburdened their souls, like a man from Kansas who wrote: "I am indebted to you for you have given me a new encouragement. I do not feel that I am doomed as our religious leaders would have me believe."

I felt gratified to think my ministry could touch a stranger in a distant place and those being hurt by insensitive, demeaning, and dehumanizing comments against homosexuality made by religious people and governmental leaders.

Seeking a Mate

I could write about homosexual culture, committed relationships, even marriage, but I didn't know how to go about finding a mate. A road map didn't exist for that. Risks and dangers would be required. Codes deciphered. The wrong move or act could land one in jail. I'm certain that many careers ended that way. Still, the need persisted. To give and receive love, experience intimacy, form a family, and make a home are basic human needs.

At first, I subscribed to beefcake magazines *The Physique Pictorial* and *The Grecian Guild Pictorial*, admiring the near-nude photographs of body builders. I wrote a column for *Grecian Guild* encouraging readers to use the same kind of discipline involved in body building to increase their spiritual lives through Bible study, worship, and the like. I half hoped a spiritually minded reader would contact me. None did.

Beefcake magazines also printed articles on health and art. George Quaintance, a male physique artist, sold original oil paintings and reproductions through such magazines. His subjects—young men dressed in jeans eyeing each other's crotches—connected with my fantasies. Through the magazine I ordered several Quaintance reproductions. Later, while visiting Manhattan, he invited me to view some original oil paintings in his room at the Chesterfield Hotel.

Quaintance was six feet tall, muscular, with perfect posture and a graceful walk and long golden blond hair styled like General Custer's. He wore tailored, Western-style clothes, silver and turquoise bracelets, necklaces, and rings. His boots shined. Entranced by his voice, smile, dress, and perfect manners, I was easily seduced. I purchased one of his paintings, "The Crusader," a portrait of a young, nude man kneeling so that his right knee rose in the foreground just high enough to cover his genitals. A crucifix hung from the sword handle the figure held in his left hand. Later, I bought another painting, "Havasu Creek." Havasu Creek was an actual location in the Grand Canyon. The painting depicted four partially nude men relaxing near a waterfall. It was his first painting to depict a young man wearing Levi's 501 jeans. I hung the paintings in my parsonage, and viewing them, dreamed of finding my mate.

Finding time away from my ministry was difficult. Time off, I realized, had to be claimed, so, except for emergencies, I began to claim Friday nights as my own. I felt like Dr. Jekyll and Mr. Hyde, given the split between the professional and personal arenas of my life, or like "The Shadow," waiting for the sun to set, waiting for Friday night, my night to cruise. Hoping to attract the attention of a man in jeans, I wore a red chambray

Western-style shirt with snap buttons left (half unbuttoned to reveal my bare chest), and tight jeans. A key ring dangled from my wide leather belt fastened in front by a large silver buckle. I wore black engineer boots. I was clueless about the signals such dress might emit. I moved quickly into my car and out of Spring Valley, hoping no one from the church would see me.

Once in Manhattan I parked near the Fifth Avenue Public Library, two blocks east of Times Square. Afraid to go to bars, I stood behind the library on a balcony that overlooked Bryant Park. There, I could see and be seen, standing or sitting on a stone railing underneath a streetlight. Men in tuxedos, jeans and boots, or business suits passed back and forth. Some hesitated. I struck up a few brief conversations and learned that the Times Square movie district was the place to go. Then I walked in and out of bushes to the end of the park on my way to Times Square.

I went inside a movie theater that smelled of stale popcorn, cigarettes, and unwashed bodies, like entrances to subways in winter. My eyes adjusted gradually to the darkness. In time, I could see dirt in the aisles and mice scurrying on the sticky floor underneath the seats. I looked for men sitting together and discovered them in the third balcony near the projection booth.

I sat two seats from the aisle to leave room for someone to sit beside me. An older man sat beside me. I moved to another row of seats, again leaving room. Another man sat beside me, but I was not attracted so I moved again. A third man sat, smelling of alcohol. Again, I moved. The seat beside me remained vacant, and on the screen Bonnie and Clyde robbed banks and eluded the law. No one else sat next to me that week.

On my third Friday night in Manhattan, a neat, clean-cut, well-mannered, professional-looking man about my age sat next to me. I left my arm on the common armrest between us and spread my right leg into his seating area. We both pretended to watch the movie, as he massaged the inside of my leg.

"Let's change clothes," he whispered.

"What?" I replied. I thought he was crazy.

"Let's change clothes," he repeated. He was serious. Strange, I thought. He must like me.

"What if the usher comes?"

"They never come up here. Come on." He took off his jeans. He wasn't wearing underwear. I was in erotic shock. His pubic hair was missing. He had a gold ring pierced through his foreskin. I gasped when I saw that: it sickened me a bit.

"Doesn't it hurt?"

"My master put it there," he said.

"What?"

"My master." I found the words strangely alluring. He kept taking off his clothes. He was almost completely nude in the movie light before I started undressing, scared to death that an usher would come. Terrified, I followed suit. Amazingly his jeans fit!

He sat there rubbing himself in my jeans and smiling. "Let's go for a drink," he said. Wearing the stranger's clothes, I imagined where threads and seams had pressed against his body, while the man beside me massaged my erection. "I want to take care of that," he said. "Let's get out a here."

We walked four blocks to his clean, orderly apartment. His furniture was new and modern. Chrome sparkled. Glass shined. Framed decorative prints gave the walls a museum-like quality. Copies of the *New Yorker* were stacked neatly on a coffee table. I noticed a wall of books. Thick carpets and exquisite drapery fabric exemplified the man's good taste, style, and financial security. I thought, at least I didn't come home with a man living in a flophouse.

We fell into a queen size bed, rolling around, our jeans pressing together. We stripped to the waist and rolled around some more. We made love.

"My name is Paul," he said afterward.

"I'm Bob," I said, trembling.

We exchanged phone numbers. "I'm a producer for the Jack Parr Show and my master is a jeweler. What do you do?" he asked.

"I'm a pastor in a church." I didn't say where.

"Really?"

"Really."

Once dressed, I was back on the street, feeling relieved, walking briskly to my car.

I much preferred the safety and privacy of a private home, but without an invitation one was left to discover love in public.

Cruising Manhattan became an impulsive search for compatibility measured by body signals. Through movie house sex encounters, I learned that wearing keys and chains on the right meant submissive, on the left, dominant. Black leather gloves and gauntlets also meant dominance. Four fly buttons on 501s told stories: one unbuttoned said, "I'm shy," two unbuttoned said, "Let's try." Sex followed physical attraction: I didn't take time to know the heart of another man, nor did the man with whom I had sex care to know me. Men came in and out of my life like a blur, impulse in search of intimacy, sometimes frustrating, but I felt like I was learning the ropes.

I didn't know how or what it would take to get "that special someone" except dressing a certain way, walking certain streets and parks, and going to Times Square movies. Months passed before I met Bob Milne at the Times Square movie house. He sat beside me, pretended to watch the movies, and said, "I like your boots and jeans. Are you into rough sex?"

"I don't know," I said.

"Next Friday, I'm hosting a party at my house on the Upper West Side." He handed me his card. "Come if you like." I noticed one of his arms was missing from the elbow down.

His house was in a row of five-story town houses. When I pushed the bell, a door opened and I walked down a long, narrow hall to another door, where I knocked and waited in anticipation. Bob opened the door, smiled and said, "Come in. Make yourself at home. Everyone else has." He led me down a flight of stairs to a basement with its ceiling removed so it was two stories high. Only a couple of construction beams were left in place.

In a corner by a two-story fireplace a young, nude man was tied, spread-eagle, to four hooks in a wall, his back pressed against rough plaster. I felt assaulted, stimulated, and repulsed at the same time. A form of fear I had never known before began to invade my nerves, yet some fascination compelled me to stay and look.

A sailor was locked with leg irons to the hearthstone, his uniform opened to reveal much of his body. As I walked by him, I noticed he had been branded on one arm by a hot poker.

Another man chained facedown on a large wooden coffee table groaned. His back bore bloody outlines from a whip. These sights took my breath away. I froze. I smelled leather, rubber, and burnt flesh. I winced when I heard a bullwhip crack in another room. Foul, abusive language filled the air. I made my way to the kitchen, where those dominating sat on chairs with those submissive who had been tied, chained, whipped, or tortured sitting on the floor at their feet or standing behind them. These were attractive, educated men in their twenties and thirties. I was too excited, afraid, confused, and amazed to remember what they might have been saying. No one spoke to me, so I wandered back into another room where a muscular man holding a pair of handcuffs walked up to me and asked, "What do you like to do?"

His question scared me. I had to get out of there. As I was leaving Bob Milne said, "Return when you can handle it."

My mind was like a kaleidoscope: curious but also a bit afraid, turned on by what I saw but thinking I might be getting into something over my head, entering a subculture for which I was not prepared. I wondered, for instance, how those men kept from escaping permanent injury or getting blood poisoning? I wondered why people in neighboring houses didn't hear moans, cries, and whacks? Memories of wounded soldiers flooded in, and I wept uncontrollably. I was confused by a concept of love so twisted as to include torture inflicted upon friends, but, inexplicably, I was drawn to it. I couldn't get to sleep for days. I kept reliving the horrible but arousing episodes in my mind. Scriptures used to judge and condemn came to mind such as Romans 1:24–25 and Romans 13:13–14:

> Therefore God gave them over in the desires of their hearts to impurity, to the dishonoring of their bodies among themselves. They exchanged the truth about God for a lie and worshiped and served the creature rather than the Creator, who is blessed forever! Amen.
>
> Let us walk decently as in the day, not in reveling and drunkenness, not in illicit sex and licentiousness, not in quarreling and jealousy. Instead, put on the Lord Jesus Christ, and make no provision for the flesh, to gratify its desires.

Paul's message, I knew from Bible study, was written from Corinth, a rowdy seaport with lots of pagan rituals. Perhaps Paul witnessed a scene like what I had observed, but within the context of worship. Was Paul warning against such behavior? I wasn't lying to God, nor did I bring my sex to church. Nonetheless, Paul's words reverberated in my mind as a warning: work this out on your own, don't follow the crowd, proceed slowly, take it to the Lord in prayer, ask for God's guidance, be faithful in Sabbath worship, don't neglect your professional duties, and think about when and where you allow yourself to experience sex. Make sexual relations an outcome of expressed affection and respect for a person.

I could not fight Paul's words any more than I could I fight my fantasies, which represented my sexual truth. If they were unpleasing in God's eyes, I would appeal to God's mercy and hope that God would understand and guide me through this maze of impulse and desire in search for a mate.

One Sexy Cowboy

In the early 1960s, if you were into leather and lived in or near New York City, you wanted to be on Frank Olson's party list. If you were on Frank's list, you could meet men: Frank had connections. I had heard about Frank's reputation, so I was pleased when he sent me a letter after my book was published. With his letter, Frank included an invitation to a party.

Frank's apartment was in a neglected frame building in a seedy neighborhood in Midtown Manhattan. On the day of the party, I squeezed into an elevator with four other men wearing boots, leather pants, jackets, and caps. Each of us carried the price of admission—a six-pack of beer. When the elevator opened, we walked through a long, narrow foyer toward a kitchen that was already clouded in a haze of cigarette smoke. Men in leather stood around the room, drinking and talking. Some groped each other. Others embraced. Many stood alone.

Too shy to speak to anyone, I leaned up against a kitchen counter, holding a beer and surveying the scene. I didn't like the taste of beer, and my eyes burned from the smoke.

I hadn't been there long when a young man approached me.

"Hi. I'm Robert Mapplethorpe," he said. "You look like you would photograph well. When you are in the mood to have any photographs taken, just give me a call." He handed me a card. "It would be great to photograph you sometime," he said, as he turned to leave. I would have been too afraid. Soon, he was introducing himself to another man.

I walked to the living room. More smoke. At least twenty men sat on cushions on the living room floor. Some talked. Others kissed. I walked around the crowded apartment, looking for someone who looked interested in me. After an hour, I was the only one who had not paired up with a partner. Some couples began to leave. Several men mentioned a new leather bar, the Silver Dollar. I left Frank's apartment to find the bar.

The Silver Dollar was dark and smoky. Standing, I ordered a beer and leaned on the bar between two men sitting on stools. I felt a hand on my rear.

"Don't turn around," a voice said.

He rubbed his hand slowly in circling motions with an occasional pinch and slap.

"Nice buns," he said to no one in particular.

I tried to see the man's reflection in the mirror but could not make out his face. He began to slap me.

"Don't move," he repeated with authority. He slapped again and again.

"This one likes his ass slapped," he said, gleefully.

I felt embarrassed but I held onto the bar. Others watched. The stranger slapped again. I had an urge to turn around and kiss that man but as suddenly as he had begun, he stopped, shifting his attention to another man with whom he repeated the routine.

Still stinging, I felt rejected by that stranger, hurt emotionally. Pathetic, I thought to myself about myself. What I wore seemed to interest others, but the person underneath the clothes felt ignored. After another hour of smoke and grope, I left. All this titillation without a lover was frustrating me. Several weeks later, I returned to the Silver Dollar to find it closed, out of business. I called Frank from a pay phone.

"Which bar is it this week?" Frank's network could literally open or shut down a bar.

"The Arcade down in the Bowery," he said.

Motorcycles were parked outside. I could barely read the tattered "Arcade" sign over the door. Curtains prevented a view inside. Windows were broken in neighboring buildings. Vagrants slept in the doorways. I watched several drunks stumble along. One walked into the Arcade and was promptly ushered out.

I entered, ordered a beer, and leaned against a wall with one boot up. Two men came in and sat at the bar in front of me. One wore jeans and a brown leather jacket with a fringe across the front and down the sleeves and a cowboy hat tilted forward to the right. What a man, I thought. I watched him through the smoke.

Our eyes met in a mirror over the bar. In a few minutes he turned around and looked me over. I didn't move. He spread his legs. I inspected him. He appeared dusty.

He stood up. He had to be six feet tall and thin. A red bandanna hung out of his half-unbuttoned shirt. He took off his jacket and draped it on the stool by the bar. He walked toward me, and I felt myself becoming hard. My leg trembled. "Please love me," I thought. He looked me in the eye and placed his left hand on the wall over my head, pressing his crotch into mine and spreading his armpit over my face. I noticed a sweat stain there, and I bit gently into the stain, tasted salt, and felt myself surrendering—wanting his next move. Suddenly, his lips were pressed against mine, and we kissed deep, wet kisses. Ecstasy.

"You're one sexy cowboy," I said.

"You're a sexy, blond stud."

"What are we going to do about it?" I asked.

"Not much tonight. I'm with a friend."

He pointed to a short man sitting at the bar.

"He's from Canada. I brought him out on the town, and I feel responsible for getting him home safely."

I was disappointed, but his concern for his friend's safety charmed me.

"What are we going to do?" I asked again.

"I'm going to stand right here against you and make love to you, if you don't mind."

"Please do, I need that," I whispered. He pressed his knee into my crotch and kissed me with an intensity that took my breath away. His hot, wet mouth pressing on mine sent exhilarating sensations throughout my body. I felt as if we were the only two men in the bar.

"You look like you've had a hard day's work," I said.

"I just came from the rodeo in Madison Square Garden. I'm helping out this week. I used to be on the rodeo circuit, but now I only work the Garden. I'm a bullwhip performer. I cut cigarettes from cowgirls' mouths and pick off silver dollars from between their fingers."

"You're a real cowboy then."

"Sometimes."

"Cowboys have always been my fantasy."

"I'm not a fantasy. I'm the real thing."

I wrapped my arms around his body and pulled him toward me.

"What's your name?" he asked.

"Bob. And yours?"

"Hugh, but the rodeo hands call me Buck because I used to ride bucking broncos."

Hugh's friend came over, and Hugh told him to order another beer, while we made a date to meet again the following week.

"Now that I have found you," I said, "there's no reason for me to hang around. I'll see you next week."

I left, thinking about the years I had been searching for a lover, wondering if I would ever see him again. I hoped I would. All week I thought about Hugh, recalling the way he looked, his kisses, his sensitive voice, and his desire to make love.

On Friday I wore the same clothes I had worn the week before. I arrived at the Arcade early. Hugh was not at the bar, nor was he standing. I fixed my eyes on the entrance, praying, "O God, don't disappoint me tonight."

Then he walked in, confident, with purpose, and stopped in the middle of the bar. There was the cowboy hat, the kerchief hanging out of the opened shirt, the jeans, and the boots. Our eyes met. "Come here, Bob," he said, with authority. He remembered my name.

"Do you want to come to my place?" I said. I could sneak Hugh in without being seen.

"Do you live alone?"

"Yes."

"Then your place is better, because my father lives with me."

"I'll drive slowly so you can follow me."

"Oh no. We'll go in my car, and you can give me directions as we go."

On the way to Spring Valley, we talked about our habits for cruising and disappointments in past relationships. I mentioned Jimmy—the man I had met at the University of Pennsylvania—and Roger—the man I had met on Fire Island. Hugh spoke of cruising Third Avenue dressed in Western clothes. He had walked slowly under the elevated subway tracks, looking in store windows, always on the lookout for another man's interest. He spoke of numerous sexual encounters but mentioned no lovers by name. I wondered if I would become just another sexual anecdote.

The next morning, we caressed, looking and smiling at each other. I noticed a tattoo—a dagger through a rose—on Hugh's arm. "Where did that come from?"

"I designed it myself when I was an art student at SMU in Dallas. The GI Bill helped pay for it."

"Is that where you joined the rodeo?"

"Yep. To earn some extra money. Is it okay if I smoke?"

"Sure. I'll get you an ashtray." I crawled back into bed, snuggled against Hugh's back, and placed the ashtray on his genitals.

"Thanks, dear," he said. Hearing that affectionate word touched me.

"Were you in the armed forces?"

"I was an airman in the South Pacific until they found out I was an artist, then I spent the rest of the war designing and painting logos and Jap flags on the sides of airplanes."

I told him about my Army days.

"I'm glad they took good care of you in the hospital."

"So am I," I said, with tears forming in my eyes. I asked him what he wanted for breakfast.

He wanted coffee and oatmeal. While I fixed breakfast, Hugh took a shower and explored the house. At the breakfast table we kept looking at each other and smiling, rubbing our legs under the table.

"I noticed your books on religion."

"I'm the pastor of a Congregational Church, and you're in their parsonage."

"I'll have to be on my best behavior," he said, smiling. "When I was a child, my mother took me to a Methodist

Church. I have fourteen years' worth of perfect attendance bars for Sunday school. I sang in the youth choir, made posters, and all that."

I asked how he made a living, and he told me that he designed training manuals and sales catalogues for a small business machine and office furniture company called Facit, Inc.

"On the weekends, I paint," he added.

"I'm glad I took my friend to the Arcade last week," he said.

"So am I. I've been looking for you for a long time."

"Me, too."

"But now I must get you back to the Bowery to pick up your car and get home or my father will begin to wonder what happened to me."

I Hope This Never Ends

During the week, I called Hugh just to hear his voice, to be reassured that he was still interested in me. In one of our conversations Hugh asked how old I was.

"Thirty-nine," I said.

"I've robbed the cradle," he said, laughing. "I'm forty-two."

The following Saturday morning, Hugh invited me to visit a friend who was remodeling an old farmhouse. As we drove in the country, Hugh talked about courses he had taken at the Brooklyn Museum Art School and the Museum of Modern Art.

"My father has never accepted the fact that I am an artist," he said.

Hugh seemed interested to know all about me, so I described my life and gave him a copy of *Christ and the Homosexual.*

The following Wednesday, he called.

"You're the first person I've met who has written a book," he said. "I enjoyed reading it. I think I will be able to relate to Christianity in more meaningful ways." This pleased me.

Two days later Hugh was back in the parsonage for another weekend. He waited at the parsonage, while I led a worship service. When I returned from church, Hugh asked, "How did it go?"

"Just fine," I replied.

During dinner, I said, "You should join us for worship: we are not so different from the Methodists, you know."

The following weekend, Hugh brought a coat and tie. That Sunday when I stood to preach, I saw Hugh's face among the parishioners. He seemed to be listening. He looked at ease. It was the first time I experienced the face of a friend looking at me from the pews.

"Good sermon," Hugh said as we ate our Sunday dinner.

"Thanks. Although preaching is my favorite pastoral activity and I prepare as best I can, when I stand before the congregation, I always feel inadequate: Who can represent the Word of God?"

"You didn't seem inadequate: just the opposite. You seemed sure of yourself, which made me believe in what you were saying."

No one in my life had ever been so interested in my work. After that, Hugh attended worship whenever he visited Spring Valley. On those Sundays he couldn't attend, I sent him a church bulletin.

Sometimes parishioners asked about the strange man.

"He's Hugh Coulter, my artist friend," I always said.

Parishioners seemed pleased by the prospect of a new member. Several even asked if Hugh might consider designing posters for upcoming church events. He was happy to oblige them.

We had known each other for about a month when I made my first trip to visit Hugh's father. On our way over I asked, "How much does he know?"

"Don't worry," Hugh answered.

Hugh's father was stocky, with a head full of thick gray hair, and bushy eyebrows on a round face. He wore glasses.

"I'd like you to meet my friend, Reverend Bob Wood, the pastor of the Spring Valley Church." Hugh said to his father.

"Are you a Mason?" Mr. Coulter said in a mellow but firm voice.

"No, but I'm a veteran," I replied.

"You are? What branch?"

"Army. Infantry. I did some fighting in Italy."

"Never liked Italians. We're Scottish. Both my parents were born there. They immigrated to Canada where I was born. Hugh tells me that you're a minister. Which denomination?"

I told him how I came to be a pastor at Spring Valley.

When I asked him what he had done before retirement, he told interesting stories about his life as the major-domo on the Leeds Estate, Plandome—some 300 acres on the North Shore of Long Island next door to the Theodore Roosevelt estate. Hugh grew up there. After a while Hugh said, "I see you two have a lot to talk about. I'll be in my studio."

"Hugh's going to make a painting," Mr. Coulter said.

"I'm going to work at it," Hugh replied as he left the room.

After Hugh left, Mr. Coulter continued to tell stories about the Leeds. He described them as "good people," and told stories about their lavish social affairs—lawn parties with tents and performers. He talked about upstairs and downstairs maids, cooks, valets, and butlers, whose work had to be coordinated. As major-domo, Mr. Coulter had to make sure everything was in order, including the transport of guests. He personally drove Anna Pavlova, Fritz Kreisler, Jan Paderewski, and other dignitaries from Manhattan to Plandome.

I was listening to living history, I thought. Mr. Coulter wasn't trying to impress me with his connections; rather, he had taken me into his confidence. The famous names he mentioned were real to his memory, and I was happy to listen to his stories about a world to which I had no access.

He explained how the Leeds used the townhouse during opera seasons, and how he drove them to the Met.

"Their season ticket included one for me in the chauffeurs' gallery, so I heard many fine operas, and all those great singers. I'll tell you something, Reverend."

"Bob is fine."

"Okay Bob. I used to carry a loaded revolver in my jacket pocket because of all the jewels Mrs. Leeds wore. Pearls were her favorite. But the Leeds were good people and generous. They provided my family with a nice house on the estate. All my staff lived elsewhere."

After a while, I felt an urge to see Hugh.

"Excuse me," I said, "but I would like to see Hugh at work."

"You'll find him on the sun porch."

Hugh, listening to classical music, faced a canvas on which he had drawn a few seemingly random charcoal lines. He was beginning to apply some color. Globs of paints lined his palette sitting on a table beside him. Beside the palette was a jar containing seven brushes of various sizes and thickness. He concentrated on the canvas, then he mixed paint on his palette. Several minutes would go by between each stroke of his wet brush on the canvas. I didn't speak.

"I find abstract painting a much freer form of artistic expression," he said. "It allows me to put myself in a painting. If I paint a red barn, everyone will have the same feeling when viewing it. But with an abstract painting, each viewer can see something different."

Around the room stood a dozen canvases in various stages of completion. As I glanced again at the canvas on Hugh's easel,

I noticed colors but couldn't discern a relationship between the colors. My eyes kept going back to one of his other paintings, a painting of a cowboy on a horse. That painting reminded me of a stained-glass window.

There wasn't much to watch—Hugh concentrating, mixing paint, and applying color to a canvas.

Later, as I prepared to leave, Mr. Coulter shook my hand and said, "I hope you are going to keep coming."

I said, "I hope so, too."

As he walked me to my car, Hugh said, "You're the first one I brought home that he's asked back."

A month later, while teaching a Vacation Church School class, I received a phone call from one of my parents' neighbors in Florida.

"Bob, I'm sorry to tell you but your father's aorta burst. He died on the way to the hospital," the caller said. "Your mother is devastated. Come as soon as you can."

I left immediately for Florida.

My brother, Harold, met me there. Harold and I escorted Mother to visit Father's body. Mother began to cry when she saw him.

"His hair is not parted correctly," she said, between sobs. "Poor Harold. His hair. That's not the way he combed his hair." Her body shook with grief and tears. "Can't somebody do something?"

"I'll try," Harold said. Harold came back with an attendant who combed my father's hair to Mother's satisfaction.

Flowers surrounded Father's casket. A few days later, we attended his funeral service. A Methodist minister described my father's faith, attention to detail, and his commitment to Sunday school. I thought about his love, how he had made me laugh, and how proud he had been of me when I came home from the war. I felt deep sadness.

After the funeral, my father's casket was shipped to Vermont. Mother, Harold, and I flew to LaGuardia where Hugh was waiting.

Hugh drove us to Spring Valley. Tired and emotionally drained, we did not say much on the trip. Like our father, Harold and I didn't talk much about our feelings. We were there to support Mother. Hugh dropped us off at the parsonage and returned home to his father.

The next day, I drove the three of us to Fair Haven, Vermont. Rain poured heavily. We remained inside my car as the pastor of the Fair Haven Congregational Church spoke a quick committal service. Mother sobbed. I held one of her hands and my brother held the other one. I said a quiet, tearful goodbye to my father:

"He's now at rest, now with Christ, free from his physical limitations and emotional turmoil. Rest," I prayed.

When I returned home, Hugh was there to greet me, to offer his condolences, and to be supportive.

"If only I could have told him about my homosexuality," I said. "His love for me would have won out over any misgivings about morality, I'm sure. But we'll have that conversation in heaven."

Hugh listened and hugged me when tears flooded my eyes. My father wouldn't have the opportunity to meet Hugh, I thought, sadly.

Soon after, with fall in the air, Hugh and I planned our first trip to the Rutland County Fair in Vermont. We wore 501s, boots, belts tooled by Hugh, and cowboy hats. On the ride up, we talked nonstop. The conversations between us were easy. After the fair, heading home in Hugh's station wagon, we pulled into a rest area. We were alone despite heavy fair traffic. Facing each other, we sat at a picnic table. With our shirts off, our legs entwined, we held hands across the table and talked. Dusk was followed by darkness.

"Let's stretch out," Hugh said.

On our backs, we watched the moon and stars. Soon we were on our sides, kissing.

"You know, I don't have the slightest desire to go to the movie houses anymore," I said.

"And I have no desire to cruise Third Avenue."

"You are just what I always wanted in a lover," I whispered. "This is my dream come true."

"I hope this never ends," Hugh replied.

We caressed each other as we talked, and became sexually aroused, kissing and feeling. Headlights appeared, and suddenly a flashlight came towards us.

"You two guys planning on spending the night here?" a state trooper shouted.

"Uh, yes sir," I replied. "Our sleeping bags are in the back of the car." I was panic-stricken.

"We've just finished supper," Hugh said. "We're enjoying your lovely Vermont air. We've been to the fair."

The trooper smiled.

"I'm pulling night duty. I'll be patrolling this stretch of highway. You two get in your sleeping bags. Nobody'll bother you."

Crickets serenaded, fireflies lit the dark sky, and Hugh and I slept together. Bliss.

A Wedding

Five months after our first meeting, Hugh came from work to the parsonage. Earlier that day in my dining room, I had draped a white dresser cloth over a low, round coffee table on which I placed two gold rings. They were identical gold rings, rough with small squares cut into the surface all around. The week before, we had shopped for those rings in a small goldsmith shop in Greenwich Village: we wanted our rings to come from a jewelry store owned by a homosexual. Beside the ring I had purchased for Hugh, I placed a book of Elizabeth Barrett Browning's sonnets. Beside the ring Hugh bought for me, I placed a book of Shakespeare's sonnets.

Again, we wore our 501 jeans, cowboy boots, leather belts, and floral pattern Western shirts. Hugh rolled his shirt sleeves halfway up his arm. The front of his shirt was unbuttoned most of the way to the navel. He looked so sexy.

We sat before the coffee table. A hanging lamp cast a soft light on the table, Hugh, and me. We sat close enough to touch. The atmosphere was serious, sacred. I felt God's presence intensely.

Although both of us had loved other men, neither one of us had ever done anything like this before. I knew that Hugh was different from anyone I had ever met. He was creative, responsible, considerate, and he seemed proud that I was a minister. I loved him and wanted to commit my life to him.

Hugh had chosen to read a sonnet from Elizabeth Barrett Browning's *Sonnets from the Portuguese.* "How do I love thee? Let me count the ways," it began. Reading the same words years later, I am convinced that Hugh somehow knew of the pain in my life that I couldn't verbalize—the awkwardness of adolescence, my loneliness as a soldier, the Igler affair, my father's disapproval of my writing, the broken relationships with men I thought I had loved, the fear of rejection I felt from my parents and parishioners. He read the sonnet, and I was deeply moved by the sincerity of his reading and the feeling of being loved.

Hugh and I looked into each other's eyes when he finished. The words had flown by so quickly. He was reading about me, about us, I thought. We held hands. I felt ecstatic. He let go of my hand, closed the book and placed it on the table beside the rings.

I picked up a book of Shakespeare's sonnets, and read, "Let me not to the marriage of true minds admit impediments; love is not love which alters when it alteration finds . . . It is an ever-fixed mark."

"That's nice," Hugh said.

I returned my book to the table. We stood and embraced, sat down again and bowed our heads.

"Bless O Lord, these rings, that he who gives it and he who wears it may abide in Thy favor all the days of our lives," I prayed.

I placed Hugh's ring on the ring finger of his left hand.

"With this ring, I thee wed, in the name of the Father, Son, and Holy Spirit," I said.

Hugh repeated those words as he placed my ring on my finger.

"Thank you, God, for bringing us together and making this evening possible," I prayed. "Help us keep the commitments we have made to sustain love between us. Keep us in Thy care. In Jesus name."

Less than ten minutes had passed. We stood again and embraced. I cannot describe the joy I felt.

After our ceremony we went into the kitchen, toasted with a glass of champagne, and went to bed. And as we slept together that night, I had the feeling that we were eternally bound.

Hugh returned home after church on Sunday. Although we talked over the telephone every day, we lived for those moments when our spoken affections could be matched with physical closeness: on weekends, vacations, and holidays. When we were together, I enjoyed just feeling Hugh's arms around my neck, and particularly savored the moments before sleep when I could see him breathing, touch him if I wanted to. Feeling him next to me was such a pleasure.

Profile Update

After eleven years of pastoral service at Spring Valley, our building expansion debts were paid, and I began to feel a need for a change. Hugh and I had been a couple for three years.

One Saturday evening, while filling out an update to my professional profile, I thought to myself, should I check "married," "divorced," or "single"? I was visiting Hugh on Long Island, waiting for Hugh's father to go to bed, waiting for Hugh to sneak into my room. We were enjoying each other's company at the end of another week. In such private moments we could talk about work, people, art, politics—anything.

"Should I check 'married'?"

"What do you mean?" Hugh said.

"We're a couple. When heterosexuals are married, friends and families celebrate their commitment. They're known as a couple. They check the 'married' box when they fill out applications."

"Our friends know us as a couple," Hugh said. "I'm satisfied with that."

"But I feel like such a hypocrite. I should check 'married' and beside the box write 'to a man.'"

"Do that and you'll never get another church," Hugh said with concern.

"But think of all the worship services, coffee hours, and potluck suppers you've attended. Sometimes I think the parishioners at Spring Valley like you more than they like me. You have such a warm way with people."

"I'm glad you think so, but they don't know, and they don't need to know."

"I know you're right. I sometimes have these terrifying dreams of walking into a trustees meeting at which I'm confronted by angry parishioners, saying, 'We know. You've lied to us, and we can't accept that from our minister.'"

"Trust those dreams," Hugh said. "The times just aren't right for our relationship to be made public. Maybe someday but not now."

"Checking single feels like a repudiation of us."

"I won't consider it a repudiation of our marriage, Bob. We've worked hard to accomplish what we have in life. Let's not throw it away. If it makes you feel better, let's agree not to talk about it unless someone asks?"

"Okay."

"And be sure to ask for an increase in salary. You deserve it."

On the new profile, under the heading Pastoral Experience, I described my ministries at Broadway Tabernacle and

Spring Valley and my work on *Christ and the Homosexual*. I indicated my interest in serving an Evangelical and Reform Church to learn firsthand about that denomination. By then the merger between Congregational/Christians and Evangelical and Reform was complete. At a national gathering, representatives from those denominations voted to take on the name the United Church of Christ (UCC). Wanting to remain near Hugh, I requested that my search for a new position be limited to the New York metropolitan area. Once completed, I mailed my profile to the denominational office that handled church placement.

Several months later, five strangers attended worship service in Spring Valley. They sat in two small groups. They were members of a search committee from the Zion United Church of Christ in Newark, New Jersey, and requested that I come to Newark to meet with the entire committee.

In February, Hugh and I drove to Newark. We found the church on Alexander Street, a busy one-way street lined with single-family homes. The parsonage, a three-story Victorian frame house, was connected to the church.

Zion's sanctuary looked European. The text on their stained-glass windows was German. I admired a small window of the head of Christ. The walls looked freshly painted. The pews and pulpit were polished, and the floor shined.

Hugh toured the parsonage while I met with the committee. Bill Morgenroth, the chairman, asked me to open the meeting with a prayer. He introduced George Gieser, an Elder, and Henry Lampus, the church treasurer.

"You might have noticed on your map that you are west of downtown Newark," Geiser said. "Our neighborhood, here, where many of our parishioners live, has always been a residential area. But I'll be honest with you Pastor, I'm afraid we're changing, and not for the good."

"I'm not sure I understand."

"Most of the men worked in the breweries," Mrs. Bilsie said. "Two breweries have closed in the past two years."

"Working class people are beginning to move out," Geiser said.

"We don't like to complain," said Mrs. Hendricks, "but after the Second World War ended, black people began to move here from the South to find work in the shipyards and docks. Our public schools now enroll more black students than white."

"The Newark public school system is the poorest in the state," Cynthia Morgenroth, a schoolteacher, said.

"Our biggest problem," Mrs. Hendricks said, "is the Mafia. They're selling drugs. I'm afraid to go downtown to shop. I'm afraid I'll get mugged."

"Women just don't carry pocketbooks on the street anymore," said Emma Bilsie.

"Now don't scare the pastor," Mr. Morgenroth said. "We all feel that Zion Church has a great future and an important role to play as a witness for Christ here in Newark."

"I'm not intimidated," I said. "You seem to be committed people. You've steadily increased your giving over the years, and your Sunday school is growing."

"But we've reached a plateau," Mr. Geiser said.

"Sometimes energy from a fresh source can help. I've learned to tackle problems, one at a time, but first, I'll want to get to know you all."

"We do things a bit differently than the Congregational Church," said Mr. Mogenroth.

"I'm willing to learn," I replied.

They asked me to leave the room, and when I returned Mr. Morgenroth asked if I would preach a sermon before the congregation. I told him I would.

On the Sunday I came to Newark to preach, I felt respected and honored. The people I met were humble. During the service, as I read from the Collect book opened on an altar (not a Communion table as had been the case at Spring Valley), I felt like a priest. When I read, the congregation was responsive. When I preached, they were attentive. When I served Communion, they took the bread and blood of Jesus, kneeling at a rail. The worship felt holy and spiritually uplifting to me, and I was glad when they voted to call me to be their pastor.

In the spring of 1965, Hugh helped me move from Spring Valley to Newark. He sewed floor-length drapes for the living room bay window and built a planter for house plants. In the dining room, he painted the built-in shelves a light cream color.

"The lighter color," he said, "is a better contrast for your glass hat collection."

He hung his paintings throughout the house. When Hugh was ready to return to his home and father, we said goodbye, hugging and kissing in a hallway not visible to anyone outside the house.

A Call to Picket

I had been in Newark a month when Dick Leitsch from Mattachine called. Since my last contact with him, Mattachine chapters had been organized in Washington, DC and Denver, and Leitsch had appeared on radio and television, in churches, and before community groups. Dr. Frank Kameny, who coordinated the Washington chapter, called for help organizing a picket at the Civil Service Building in Washington to protest the practice of summarily firing gay people.

I called Hugh and explained the details.

"He has the necessary permits, and hopes to conduct an orderly, peaceful demonstration," I said. "He doesn't expect problems, but an ACLU attorney will be on hand, just in case."

"If you want to participate, Bob, I'll be there with you. Do you think the picket will be televised?"

"I don't know."

"What if your parishioners see you on television?"

"I'll just explain that ministers have taken to the picket lines to promote civil rights for other minorities, and I feel that the rights of homosexuals should also be protected. I guess I'm ready to take that risk.

"But what about your colleagues at work?"

"They aren't that civic-minded. If they happen to see a story about the picket in the newspaper or on television, I'll just tell 'em it was my day off and I can do as I please."

Craig Rodwell, who would later open the Oscar Wilde Memorial Bookstore in Greenwich Village, Dick Leitsch, Hugh, and I rode together to Washington. On the way down, Leitsch talked about the significance of what we were about to do.

"We'll be making the point that the Constitution exists for gays," he said. "Perhaps future gays will look upon June 25, 1965, as a historic day in the way that blacks think of Selma."

In Washington, we joined fifteen other men in coats and ties and seven women in skirts and blouses. I was the only clergy in the group, and I wore my clerical collar.

Holding our signs, we walked in a circle on the plaza of the Civil Service Building. Afraid of what might happen, my adrenaline pumped. I imagined government officials confronting us, and passersby calling us names. We walked for two hours. Hugh snapped pictures. Police watched. Several cloak-and-dagger type characters observed and photographed us from parked cars and from across the park.

After the picket, we rode home recounting the day's events. "I'm not sure that our picket has accomplished much," I said.

"It's not over," Leitsch said. "We've much work to do. What's happening in your denomination?"

"Not much," I said.

"You have to make it happen," he said.

"How?"

"Write letters. Make demands."

"I'm busy with my church work," I said.

"There's always time to write a letter." I felt guilty.

The Newark newspapers did not cover the picket of the Civil Service Building in Washington, nor did the local television or radio news broadcasts. A picture of me holding my sign did appear on the cover of the next issue of *The Ladder*, a lesbian magazine. No one in my church heard about the picket. They had their own concerns to consider.

Ministry in Newark

I began my ministry in Newark the same way I had in Spring Valley, attending church meetings and making home and hospital visits. Soon, I was familiar with the core group, all German immigrants.

Hugh, inspired by the devotion and commitment of the Zion Church members and wanting to be supportive of my ministry, moved his church membership from Spring Valley to Newark. As he had in Spring Valley, he helped church committees decorate for parties, donated paintings for fundraisers, and took photographs behind the scenes. He washed dishes at the semi-annual sauerbraten dinner. During Advent, he led a workshop on the art of wreath and candle making and creative gift-wrapping. He designed and printed covers for our newsletters. He often attended worship, staying for coffee hours. They seemed to accept him as a bachelor friend of mine and even elected him as a delegate to the Conference Annual Meeting.

At the Zion Church, parishioners approached their obligations in a serious, respectful manner. Committees had different names. For instance, deacons at Zion served the same function as trustees at Spring Valley. What I had known to be deacons, they called elders. Most parishioners addressed me as "Herr Pastor." They held my vocation in high regard, and I felt put on a pedestal. Worship featured more liturgies. Elders assisted during Communion, which was served five times a year instead of once a month. Zion's confirmation class was more extensive than Spring Valley's had been. Beginning at age twelve, students spent two years (as opposed to eight months at Spring Valley) learning the Heidelberg Catechism, Bible, and church history. At Zion one could always feel a connection to the Old World and the thread of Christian history that came from Europe to America with the immigrants.

During home visits, senior members told stories about how Newark had given them a chance for a new life in America. They spoke of their mother church, St. Stephen's, in downtown Newark, the streetcars they once rode, and the beer breweries where they had worked. They told how they had settled in beautiful, safe Vailsburg—named for the farmer who had owned the land—to build a mission church. They described the changes to the neighborhood and their fear of vandalism to the church property or being mugged. They worried their children would move to escape the poor schools, drugs, and crime. They reminisced about their childhood days walking to church and attending a thriving Sunday school.

Racial tensions were growing. Local news featured reports of substandard housing and disinterested landlords, crime, unemployment, and high maternal and infant mortality. Many of Newark's white elected officials, school administrators, police, and fire officers kept voting addresses in the city but commuted to suburban residences. Negotiations between Black leaders and city officials often failed to produce results. As tensions mounted in the community, parishioners became fearful, and with good cause.

One morning our church secretary, Mildred Andrewski, a mother of two, arrived at church disarrayed and crying hysterically. Her face was bleeding.

"What happened?" I asked.

"I was mugged, and they took my purse."

With a wet towel I wiped the blood off her face and hands, saying, "You're safe now." Her cuts and bruises did not look severe.

"Maybe we should call the police."

"If you do, they'll be waiting for me. I'll be all right. They didn't get much."

We walked together and I waited for her to lock her front door. As I walked back to the church, I was aware of being alone and a little frightened for my safety. I noticed the church—neatness and orderliness in a chaotic community—and felt pride. Their building and deeply felt religious traditions were helping parishioners cope.

In the summer of 1967, rumors of militants moving to Newark spread, increasing the fear of violence. Mayor Hugh Addonzio minimized the threat, but Italian vigilantes met regularly to plan actions against potential troublemakers.

One hot day in July a Black cab driver was, according to news reports, beaten to death by Newark police. Protests against police brutality ensued. A demonstration at the Newark police station erupted into a riot. Snipers, from rooftops and apartment windows, shot randomly. Looters raided local businesses. The National Guard and state troopers joined the city police in exchanging gunfire with snipers and arresting lawbreakers. Armed checkpoints were established, and curfews were enforced. Wearing my clerical collar, I walked Alexander Street hoping to minister to those in the community that might have need and reassure and calm my parishioners.

The riots stopped just five blocks from the church. Five days of violence produced fifteen million dollars in damages, 1,300 arrests, 1,200 injuries, and twenty-five deaths—twenty-three Black people and two white people. Broken glass was everywhere, and blood stained the sidewalks.

Following the riots, a group of clergy—a Roman Catholic priest, a Jewish rabbi, a Lutheran minister, a Presbyterian minister, and myself—worked to establish a community ministry in a vacant Methodist Church building. We hired youth and prenatal counselors, and two nurses, one specializing in public health and the other for home visits. We enlisted teachers to offer courses in home ski and recruited members of our churches as volunteers to staff drop-in centers for youth and women, host movie nights and teenage dances, and prepare food baskets for distribution. For funding, we wrote grants and appealed to our local congregations for support.

But the community continued to change. White families moved out of the area. Single-family houses were converted into two- and three-family units. Drug pushers openly sold their goods near the church. Parishioners began to feel overwhelmed, helpless.

To help bolster my parishioner's faith, I organized a tour of the Holy Land. Parishioners from Spring Valley and Zion attended seminars in which I lectured on the geography of the Bible, Muslim architecture, and Middle Eastern religious customs, and Hugh introduced Arab and Greek Art. I created an itinerary and booked transportation and hotel accommodations. Hugh signed on as the tour photographer.

The following spring, we landed in Rome and toured catacombs—claustrophobic, dark, and narrow alleyways connecting chambers littered with skulls—where persecuted Christians had lived. On Mount Tabor, a Franciscan Monk made a speech about Christ's Transfiguration. We visited Mars Hill in Athens, where the Apostle Paul had preached his Sermon to an Unknown God. At Sychar in Samaria, inside an Orthodox church filled with icons lit by burning candles, we stood around a dark hole—Jacob's Well. We rode horses to Petra, a city carved in rock, fiery red in the sun's light. Jerusalem was our final stop.

After touring the city, we concluded our day in the Upper Room, just outside the Old City wall. We climbed worn limestone steps and entered a former mosque where a niche in a wall pointed towards Mecca. A limestone floor was all that remained of the actual Upper Room—the place where the Last Supper was eaten just before Jesus was arrested; the place where his disciples hid and awaited the day of Pentecost, where Jesus reappeared after His resurrection, where Thomas said, "I won't believe unless I touch him," where the Christian church was born. The room was empty except for columns. Hugh examined the columns and found color under the whitewash—coats of arms painted by Crusaders during the twelfth and thirteenth centuries. Suddenly, led by the Holy Spirit, I took down the rope railing intended to keep people out. I read a liturgy from my prayer book, and spoke the words of our Communion Sacrament, offering up a chalice borrowed from the hotel and bread from our lunch. We were overwhelmed by the presence of the Holy Spirit. Everyone felt it.

At night, Hugh and I shared a hotel room. We talked about the incredible fruits of faith in Christ, something you could not see, yet offering so much in terms of hope and love. And we discussed the spiritual growth visiting where Jesus lived and experiencing first-hand the landscape and historic sites important in the history of Israel and early Christianity. As I drifted off to sleep, after goodnight kisses and words of endearment, I quietly thanked God for bringing such a spiritual, creative man into my life.

Another night, Hugh shared concerns that his father's health was in decline. Hugh doubted his abilities to care for him.

Later that year, Hugh moved his father to a nursing home. Hugh's father did not fight the move, but after the move he gave up. He became weaker and weaker, and on his ninetieth birthday died in his sleep. Hugh mourned his passing, and I tried to be supportive by listening, consoling, and conducting the funeral services.

Meanwhile, the Zion Church continued to be vandalized, and its members mugged. A church vote cancelled evening church meetings. Parishioners repainted and replanted flowers. They kept coming to church. Although the number of parishioners remained about the same, they were older. Our confirmation class numbers dwindled. My last one had two pupils.

I began to think of the Zion Church as one with a glorious past and an uncertain future.

"God is with us," I repeated often, trying to encourage hope. "Your faith and church life has brought you this far."

No matter how much they believed in me, I knew I could not stop the transitions that were taking place, nor could I return them to the time when their church was so vital and full of people.

Faithful Workers in the Vineyard

The United Church of Christ (UCC) ministry most involved in justice and equality was the Board for Homeland Ministries (BHM). Dick Leitsch from Mattachine challenged me to press denominational officials to consider the needs of homosexuals. The BHM seemed like a good starting point. Leitsch said: "You must identify the people in power and convince them to take you seriously. The important thing is persistence: Don't give up. Look for action, not talk." Serving the larger church was consistent with my goals in ministry, so I informed the Central Atlantic Conference staff that I was interested in serving on the corporate board for the BHM. They recommended me. Parishioners at the Zion Church in Newark considered my appointment an honor. My term began in 1968.

When I began my term, race, urban issues, and equality for women were favored priorities. BHM executives did all they could to keep up with these demands. However, I sought to add the needs of homosexuals. I encouraged them to think about and develop a ministry for homosexuals. I thought they might include articles on the subject in their publications or produce training for clergy who did not feel equipped to respond to the needs of homosexuals. Since I didn't feel safe discussing the subject within my congregation, I felt a certain relief writing to these colleagues in distant places. I would be open to their ideas and send them information.

When the Quakers in England published *Towards a Quaker View of Sex* in which they described homosexuality as "natural," I sent them a copy. When Norman Pittenger's book *Time for Consent* was published, I sent reviews. When the North American Conference of Homophile Organizations met under the banner, "Gay is good," I sent copies of newspaper articles about the event. Through my letters, I also described the work of Mattachine, passing along articles from Mattachine publications. I wrote about the Council on Religion and Homosexuals organized by the United Methodist's Glide Urban Center in San Francisco.

In 1966, Keith Wright from the National Council of Churches organized an interdenominational study seminar on the church and homosexuals in White Plains, New York. Thirty-six people—theologians, denominational staff, pastors, psychiatrists, psychologists, lawyers, and representatives from Mattachine Society and Daughters of Bilitis—attended. Alexander Harper, from the New York Office of CCSA, also came. After the gathering, Harper met with me before writing his report describing the seminar and its outcomes for CCSA, which included, "While recognizing the demonic possibilities in sex as in any human power, we believe that the time has come in the church and in American life to affirm homosexuality no longer as a crime, as in law, no longer as sickness, as in medicine, and no longer as sin, as in the church, but as an acceptable variation of normality."

He also suggested to his CCSA colleagues that an issue of *Social Action* be dedicated to exploring homosexuals and the church. I felt encouraged.

Meanwhile Lewis I. Maddocks, from the CCSA office in Washington, had been writing to me of his interest in the law and homosexuals. He requested names of Mattachine leaders with whom he could correspond. He seemed engaged by my concerns. It's a beginning, I thought.

Truman Douglass, from BHM, had a different response. He wrote of his reluctance to expand BHM's program to include a ministry to homosexuals, citing budget limitations, and he reminded me that the BHM had helped fund a ministry to homosexuals in San Francisco.

A week earlier, like most UCC pastors across the country, I had received a letter from Douglass expressing the Board's concern for "intra-community conflict," no doubt a response to the riots in Newark, Watts, and other cities. He warned of the consequences of suppressing the symptoms of unrest while leaving the causes untouched. He compared the "breakdown and disaster" in our American cities with the famine in India and war in the Middle East. He wondered if the church could "make a difference." He requested that I share the "content and urgency" of his letter with my congregation.

I sympathized with and admired Douglass's concern for the millions of citizens living in ghettoes. I supported his effort to raise money to help disenfranchised people develop capacities for self-determination. I shared his concerns with my congregation and took up the offering. Soon after, I received a copy of "Homosexuality as a Christian Ethical Problem," a speech by Rev. Ralph Weltge, the BHM executive for young adult's ministry. Weltge's speech had been delivered at a YMCA Forum in Philadelphia. In his speech, Weltge criticized my book.

"Homosexuality," he wrote, "is a bizarre sexuality. No matter how the behavioral scientists slice it up, the Christian faith is against the phenomena in all its forms and degrees. . . . When a man is a Christian, he cannot become a homosexual."

Instead of finding support from BHM, my book was criticized, with no opportunity for rebuttal. Homosexuals, I felt, were being attacked. Glad to see the justice-seeking vein of the church affirming women and African Americans, I wrote Douglass to express my disappointment in the apparent lack of concern for developing a ministry with homosexuals and to take issue with Weltge's paper. I requested a meeting.

Douglass responded by offering a meeting date and criticisms of what he called my "violent" and "intemperate" attack on Weltge, calling it a "diatribe" and "intensely personal." He wrote of his agreement with Weltge's opinions and accused me of failing to deal with the content of his paper.

Douglass's defense of Weltge further offended me. I felt I wasn't being taken seriously. Even though my homosexuality was still concealed, I felt that I was being judged and condemned by heterosexual men.

Seven BHM staff (all men) met with me in Douglass's office. I read from a written statement, as they politely listened. I recounted my understanding of statistics and needs as I had described them in my book. They asked few questions, and when the hour was up, I thanked them for their attention. As I was putting on my coat in the outer office, I heard laughter coming from the meeting room. I left feeling put down and discouraged.

In 1967, another event occurred: a CCSA issue of *Social Action* devoted to civil liberties and homosexuality was published. Its editor, Elizabeth Johns, called to tell me the printing date.

When I asked her if I might see a copy before it was distributed, she invited me to her office.

Holding and reading those forty-eight pages felt exhilarating. In an article entitled, "The Homosexual and the Law," Maddocks had written, "The church has failed at the most basic level in its dealings with the homosexual by failing to recognize him as a human being who is sacred in the sight of God." I almost cried. He proposed many of the recommendations for ministry I had suggested in *Christ and the Homosexual* and recommended *Towards a Quaker View of Sex* for further study. In the article, "A New Frontier for Freedom," Dick Leitsch described Mattachine's efforts to "fight, struggle, and litigate to gain equality under the law." Daniel Day Williams, a professor of theology at Union Seminary, had written an article comparing several books (including mine) about homosexuality and religion, concluding that sex "is a mystery in the full Christian sense of that term which should be openly and freely discussed in love and honesty."

The following year Maddocks wrote to me about a planning meeting in Cleveland where he saw Douglass "become more sympathetic." He was encouraged by two developments: a consultation attended by those responsible for whatever corporate action the UCC would take in this area, and news of the preparation of a resolution for General Synod on some of the legal reforms which Truman Douglass said BHM would support. He then addressed me personally:

> Let me talk politics for a minute. What you wish the church to do now will not be done even in the near future. Those who can do something resent being pushed faster than they think the church should go. This is not the civil rights problem in which everyone knows what the injustices are and what ought to be done about them. This is a situation, like it or not, in which those in positions of church leadership may not yet be aware of the extent

> of injustices to homosexuals, nor do they agree on what should be done even about those injustices they realize do exist. What I am trying to say, Bob, is that you have created resistance rather than cooperation because those you would like to see move are convinced that nothing short of "homosexual justice now" is acceptable. I have heard more than one person say, "You can never satisfy Bob Wood." I guess, Bob, what I am trying to say is that you have to accept people where they are and be patient with their attempts, no matter how feeble, to understand a problem which to them is far more complex than it is to you. I know it is easier for me to feel this way because I have not been fighting this battle as long as you have, so forgive me for what may well be colossal naiveté.

I welcomed such an honest letter, but I was feeling more determined to see my denomination respond to my concerns. That year, while the Metropolitan Community Church called for gays and lesbians to leave churches that were unwelcoming, CCSA supported a motion before General Synod calling for the repeal of laws that made private relations between consenting adults a crime. Nothing happened. Synod voted to focus on "peace" and "the urban crisis." Later, Maddocks wrote:

> I brought the matter up before a subcommittee of the Report Committee on the CCSA and ran into resistance. It took the usual form of: "I'm not against your concern, but we'll never get General Synod to move in this direction." How much longer this procrastination will last is hard to say. One thing I am sure of is that it will continue until the problem becomes visible and in some kind of pressure comparable to that represented by the actions of James Forman. I still think nothing significant is going to happen until the millions of homosexuals in the U.S. are willing to contribute a dollar a year to an action organization. The potential for mass education and political action is there if it could only be stimulated. This doesn't mean that

> I've given up—I haven't. I'm just reminding you of the response for all the emphasis on support for Blacks and so little in support for the homosexual community. Take the American Indian—that issue is not one that requires much education—because nearly everyone agrees that they have had a raw deal and ought to be helped, but even so, virtually nothing is being done in this problem area.

My efforts, Maddocks' research and writing, the work of the Conference on Religion and Homosexuality in San Francisco, and church publications were not producing the needed ministry. What would it take? Should I try to work for change within the UCC or abandon it for MCC? At times, I felt tempted to do just that. At Mattachine, I met others from mainline denominations asking the same question. Seeking to find support and learn from one another, we organized the First National Conference on Religion and the Homosexual at the Interchurch Center in New York City. During my keynote address, I felt as if I was preaching to the converted. National instrumentalities, we agreed, should be listening to homosexuals rather than pontificating about them.

Soon after, Robert Moss became president of the UCC. Moss had accompanied one of my groups on a Bibleland tour and had become acquainted with Hugh and me as a couple. I felt I knew him, so I called him. As a gesture of support, he assigned a four-man committee to study homosexuality and the church. A year later, I discovered the committee had not met. I was becoming angry.

Howard Spragg replaced Truman Douglass as the new BHM executive vice president. For two years, I wrote to Spragg requesting that homosexual concerns be placed on an agenda our corporate meetings. It didn't happen, so I wrote a paper, entitled, "I Accuse," listing my perceptions of the BHM's "indifference" to gays and lesbians. I wrote that homosexuals and their needs were absent from the pages of the Christian education resources, save one book published by The Pilgrim Press. Seminaries didn't offer classes on the topic. Conference staff and pastors weren't being trained to minister to them. The hiring policies of the BHM and the corporations and governments with whom they were invested needed to be reviewed. I mimeographed two hundred copies, which I left on a literature table near the entrance of the meeting hall in Baltimore.

During the meeting, an African American clergyman, one of the program leaders, approached me and asked if I would speak to the assembly if he could arrange it.

A vote was taken, and I stood at the podium and read my paper.

My statements were included in the minutes, along with a notice of our next meeting in Florida and a letter Spragg wrote listing BHM's accomplishments on behalf of homosexuals. The Pilgrim Press had published *The Same Sex*. Five other books and two units in the UCC curriculum focused on sexuality. "Although neither of these units deal explicitly with homosexuality," Spragg wrote, "the basic learning theory behind the total UCC curriculum is one built strongly on the notions of empathy and dialogue and the full acceptance of all persons." He listed ministries the BHM supported: the Council on Religion and the Homosexual and a Night Ministry in San Francisco, and Urban Young Adult Action which has a strong concern for ministries with the homosexual young adult. "Almost all our new church development pastors report counseling and aiding homosexuals in the communities where they reside," he also wrote. "Further, our efforts through United Ministries in Higher Education are rather extensive. Campus ministers do a great deal of work with and for homosexuals." He assured me that the BHM had no hiring policy concerning homosexuals and, as far as he knew, had never discriminated against homosexuals in their hiring practices.

I wrote a letter demanding another meeting to discuss my concerns. An unproductive meeting followed. Later, I wrote my reactions to Spragg:

> Racial Justice NOW, but the homosexual can wait. I heard lots of reasons why certain things could not be done. I heard no one say, 'Let's give this or that a try!' While the atmosphere was not hostile, it was certainly negative. Millions of gays in America are calling out to the Church and as yet it hasn't replied with much of a positive creative redemptive message.

Meanwhile, perhaps inspired by Stonewall (the three-day riot in June 1969, in which gays fought with raiding police in a Greenwich Village gay bar) impatience, anger, or pride, gay men and lesbians began to talk about "coming out." Jim Foster addressed the 1972 Democratic National Convention. Dr. Bruce Voeller formed the National Gay Task Force. Kathy Kozachenko was elected to the Ann Arbor (Michigan) city council. Elaine Nobel was elected to the Massachusetts State Legislature. Minnesota State Senator Allan Spear came out. Leonard Matlovich, having come out, was discharged from the Air Force. Harvey Milk was elected to the San Francisco Board of Supervisors and was later assassinated. Jerry Brown appointed Stephen Lachs to State Superior Court. Between fifty thousand and a hundred thousand lesbians, gay men, and supporters marched on Washington. Homosexuality was removed from the American Psychiatric Associations diagnostic manual of mental disorders. In 1971, I received a letter from Bill Johnson, a young seminarian in California seeking ordination within the UCC as an openly gay man: "I have realized that the validation of my ministry does not come from ordination but rather from the affirmation of those among whom I minister. I conceive of myself as a minister already . . . the official ordination by the church, to me, is more of a recognition of my ministry than a validation of it. Nevertheless, I will pursue the course to ordination. I'm trying to prepare myself psychologically and emotionally for the worst with regard to the final decision, but I refuse to be rendered hopeless until the Ecclesiastical Council or the Conference on Church and Ministry announces a negative decision. Even then, I will find a way to give my ministry even though it will not be recognized by the United Church of Christ officially. I know too much about the suffering of gay people in our society, the suffering of blacks, Chicanos and Indians, too much about the suffering of women, to be deterred by institutional narrowness from the ministry to which I know in my heart God has called me."

On June 25, 1972, representatives from the Golden Gate Association and Northern California Conference assembled with members of the Community UCC in San Carlos, California, to ordain Bill Johnson. Rev. Johnson soon organized a gay presence for General Synod. Having organized a Gay Caucus, he sent letters encouraging homosexuals within the denomination to join him "out of the closet."

Perhaps Rev. Johnson knew how I had concealed my sexuality in my writing and public speeches. He didn't judge, nor did he criticize. He knew nothing about the layers of fears and apprehensions created for me by hearing McCarthy's accusations or news of police raids or people losing their jobs or being labeled as sick by the psychological community. He knew little of the resistance to a ministry for homosexuals I experienced from my own denomination. I was happy for Johnson, curious to see how his ministry would evolve. For so long, I had feared the consequences of having my homosexuality discovered. I never stopped to think about the consequences of life in the closet. Such considerations would come much later.

Maynard

Despite my best efforts, after nine years at the Zion Church in Newark, the congregation stopped growing and their resources were stretched. I felt incapable of reversing the trends. I began to think that a new pastor might bring fresh energy and new approaches. I also grew tired of living in a neighborhood so unsafe that my mother wouldn't visit.

I updated my profile on which I checked the "single" box once more in the hope of improving my odds for placement. And I enlarged the geographical search area to include New England. UCC placement professionals warned me that white male clergy over the age of fifty could be difficult to place.

After several years without a response—not even an interview—I became discouraged. Perhaps word was out that I was gay.

Naturally I was thrilled and anxious when, in 1978, I received a call from a search committee from the Union Congregational United Church of Christ in Maynard, Massachusetts. They read my profile and requested an interview.

The Union Church, located on a hill, with its white clapboard exterior, reminded me of the church I attended as a child in Fair Haven, Vermont. One of the search committee members showed me the parsonage, a split-level house on a dead-end street about a mile from the church. The streets between the parsonage and church were lined with well-kept homes and gardens. Drivers and pedestrians in town were courteous. Crime was low, the sound of sirens infrequent. I hoped and prayed that my pastoral skills and the congregation's needs would be a match.

Several search committee members expressed a concern for thoughtful worship, pastoral visitation, and a commitment to build a Sunday school program. Others named pastoral turnover as a pressing concern. Two previous ministers had left after a short time. Desiring continuity, they asked if I would be willing to remain at the Union Church for ten years. I said I would.

I was delighted when the committee decided to have me preach a sermon before the congregation. After the sermon, the congregation voted unanimously to call me as their pastor.

I began my ministry in Maynard the same way I had at Spring Valley and Newark—by visiting parishioners. Union members were mostly white, upper middle-class families employed by Digital Equipment Corporation. Many talked about the prosperity of the times—Digital's growth and soaring real estate values. They talked about investments, their children's education, and strategies for church growth. They seemed relatively uninterested in life beyond their community.

I missed the folks at the Newark church and our gay friends in Newark and Manhattan. My only acquaintance outside the parishioners at the Union Church was Kay Mitchel, who lived in Shirley Center, a few miles from Maynard. Years before, I saw her name in magazines advertising glass hats for sale. She had a formidable collection. Hugh and I had visited her several times, and she had always been gracious. Now that I was in Maynard, I visited her more often. She was always a perfect hostess, cordial and warm.

My mother was so taken by my descriptions of the Union Church and the town of Maynard that she immediately made plans to visit. She had sold her house in Florida and was living in a three-room apartment connected to my brother's house in Newport News, Virginia.

Hugh and I adjusted to the physical distance between us by reminding ourselves how we would be together as often as possible on weekends and during vacations. We were glad to have telephones, which allowed us to talk every other day.

"How are you?" I asked one day after I had been in Maynard for about two months.

"I'm busy with work," he said.

"How's your painting coming along?"

"No time or energy. To tell you the truth, I'm thinking of you all the time."

"I miss you too, but I keep busy visiting parishioners, and I'm making plans for mother's visit. I sure hope you can come soon."

"I think that can be arranged," he said. "You are not going to believe what has happened."

"Try me."

"Facit has been bought, and the new company is bringing its own art department. I've been offered an early retirement package."

"What exactly does this mean?"

"It means I'm going to sell my house on Long Island and look for a house close to you, one with an attached barn to make a studio."

"When are you coming to look?"

"Perhaps I'll come when your mother leaves so that you'll have time to drive me around."

"Great," I said, happy in thoughts of Hugh living nearby and our spending time together, which would be easier than ever with Hugh retired.

Mother arrived soon after, looking older and a little unsteady as an eighty-three-year-old.

"Such a large house for one person," she said repeatedly.

She enjoyed seeing the antiques, some of which had belonged to her and my father. I wanted to spoil her a little. Each evening, I set the dining room table and served dinner, but she insisted on washing the dishes. She spoke often about my brother and his wife Jane and their two children. She didn't ask about Hugh, even though his paintings hung on walls throughout the parsonage. However, I told her about his plans to buy a home with a barn near Maynard.

"What does he need a barn for?"

"We'll turn that into a studio and gallery for his paintings."

"Oh," she said, uninterested.

On those days when I called on parishioners in the hospital and nursing homes or attended meetings, mother watched television and wrote letters. Occasionally, parishioners, knowing my mother was alone during the day, stopped by.

Her week with me flew by and as she boarded a plane to return home, she said with feeling, "I sure enjoyed my visit with you."

"Me too," I said.

I enjoyed Mother's friendly greetings at the end of the day. She had been eager to hear all the details of my day. I was happy for the time with her.

The following week, when Hugh stepped off a Greyhound bus, we were so eager to see and touch each other that we hugged in public.

Hugh was eager to look for a house, so we started that afternoon. During our three weeks together, we saw many houses that held no interest for us. But when the agent pulled into the driveway of a house in Pepperell, Hugh gave me a thumbs up before we reached the front door.

By October he had moved to Pepperell and joined the Maynard church. I gave Hugh's telephone number to the church secretary in case of an emergency so I could drive to see Hugh on Friday mornings and stay through Saturday afternoon. Free from the danger of a parishioner dropping in unannounced, we felt more privacy there. On Sundays, Hugh attended church where I introduced him to curious parishioners as my artist friend. Monday through Thursday, I did my church work while Hugh renovated his house.

Other weekends found us on rides in the country, looking for a new restaurant or antiques shop or art supply store. We also visited the Brimfield Antique Show, and set up at art shows, like the one on the Village Green in Townsend, Massachusetts, where Hugh displayed his paintings on easels.

Beside the easels, on a small table he placed a photo album filled with colored slides of paintings hanging in his gallery at home. We sat in lawn chairs watching the crowds pass by, waiting for someone to express interest in his work.

One day Hugh found Priscilla Jane Stevens Scheibel, who called herself PJ, sitting beside her paintings, wearing a long flowing skirt and a large brim hat. She had a colorful scarf around her neck. I asked if I could take her picture, and she struck a wonderful pose. I told her that I would send her a copy if it came out well.

When the photograph was ready, Hugh and I took it to her. A bubbly, tall, thin, thirty-five-year-old, wearing a loose-fitting cotton dress and low-heeled shoes, greeted us at the door. She bore a strong resemblance to Hugh: they could have been siblings. “I’m a decorative artist,” she explained as we looked through her portfolio—photographs of painted gardens in foyers, on exterior bathroom windows, and on furniture.

“I want to read your palms to see if you’re compatible,” she said.

“Look here,” she said to me. “Your lifeline. It’s broken. Let me see the other hand. It’s broken, too; you must have had a near-death experience to have your lifeline broken on both hands.”

She talked about the healing qualities of pyramids and crystals. I didn’t know what to think. She showed us her garden. She began to visit Hugh during the week, and the three of us became friends.

Soon after we met PJ, Mother wrote that Harold and Jane would be moving from Newport News to Williamsburg, and that Jane’s mother would be coming to live with them.

“I don’t know how I’m going to like the new arrangement,” she added.

A Stroke

In early December 1979, Hugh and I cut down a large balsam at a local Christmas tree farm and placed it in Hugh's living room in front of a bay window facing the driveway. We were celebrating our second Advent season in Hugh's house. Hugh played Christmas music, which reminded him of his childhood.

Over the years we collected many antique ornaments, each containing a special memory for us. I took them out of their boxes, one at a time: a china Santa, a tiny brass bugle, a glass angel with cotton wings, red and green balls with jingles inside, a small glass chalet, and many more. Hugh hung them on the tree, sometimes moving them two or three times before he was satisfied that they were hanging in the right place.

"Plug in the lights," Hugh said as he adjusted the star atop the tree.

I bent over, inserted the plug, and looked up. Before I could react, Hugh had fallen into the tree, which slammed into the bay window. Ornaments smashed! Hugh lay on the floor.

When I grabbed Hugh's arm to help him up, his body was dead weight. I gently laid him back on the floor.

"What am I doing down here?" he said, looking bewildered. "I'll get out of the way and get up."

He tried to get up again but couldn't use his limp left arm and leg.

"We had better get you to the doctor," I said.

I picked up his shoulders and leaned him against the couch.

I gathered our coats, Hugh's wallet, my car keys, and quickly pulled my car up to the front porch. Using a dining room chair for support, I helped Hugh to his feet and draped his coat over him. He leaned on me. I held him tightly around the waist. We were tangled, God only knows how we managed to walk to the car.

"Where are we going?" he said. "I want to sit down."

"I'm taking you to the hospital."

Several attendants helped me take Hugh into the emergency room. I presented Hugh's wallet and medical card to the hospital receptionist, who filled out the forms. No one asked who I was. They wheeled Hugh away, and I waited in the reception area. I felt like crying: I wanted to be by his side.

After a while, a nurse came to me to say that they were going to keep him in the hospital, and that I could visit him in his room.

Holding his right shoulder, I leaned over him. I wanted to kiss him but settled for a squeeze of his right hand. He was almost asleep, so he didn't reply.

I felt so sad, alone, and helpless to do anything for him. On my way home and later, when the uneasiness in the pit of my stomach turned to tear-producing panic, I prayed, "Be with him Lord. Hold him for me. Comfort him. Let him know I'm thinking of him."

The next morning, I returned with his reading glasses, a robe, some art and rodeo magazines, and his electric razor.

"They tell me I've had a stroke," he said. "See, my left arm and leg won't move. A therapist is supposed to come in. They told me I was lucky that it hadn't spread and that I'll probably regain the use of my arm and leg. But I still don't know how I got here. Did you bring me, Bob?"

"Yes, dear. We were putting up our Christmas tree. Don't you remember?"

I told him the story.

"Oh, is that what happened? I hope I didn't break any of our ornaments. I'm dying for a cigarette."

Although he was hospitalized less than a week, I wanted to be with him more often than I could. The Advent season was a busy time: poinsettias to be ordered, the sanctuary to be decorated, Sunday school programs, Christmas parties, special services, decorating the parsonage, hosting an open house, buying gifts, and sending cards. I could not visit Hugh every day, but we talked on the telephone, and he would describe his work with the physical therapist or visits he received.

Hugh's strength gradually returned, first to his arm and then to his leg, but his hip and lip remained paralyzed. Although he drooled and limped, he could paint. On Christmas Eve, he came to the parsonage for dinner. We exchanged gifts and telephoned friends, then I drove him back to Pepperell.

Soon after, Mother made her second visit to Maynard. After church one Sunday she said a lady had asked her why she didn't move in with me.

"Are you thinking you would like to move here?" I asked.

"If I were here, I would have more privacy," she said.

"I thought you had your own room and bath."

"Harold and Jane are so nice to have me but I'm really feeling cramped," she said. "There's not enough space in my room for a TV, and the programs they watch are not the ones I'm interested in."

"I thought you liked it there."

She became quiet.

I told Hugh about Mother's wish to move in with me.

"Remember my father," he said. "I could seldom do anything right in his eyes. Prepare yourself."

"I'm mostly concerned with how her living with me might cut into the time we have together."

"Does she know we sleep together, or does she think I sleep in the guest room?"

"I don't know."

Fearing her rejection, I never discussed our relationship with her.

"It's your decision," he said.

I had always believed that parents should be honored. Throughout my life, mine had given me much without making demands. It was time to give something back. If Mother wanted to live in Maynard, I would honor her desire. She seemed pleased when I told her she could move in with me.

Hugh responded to the news in a practical way. During the winter months, in the guest room at the parsonage, he stripped old wallpaper, painted the walls a cheerful yellow, and hung new drapes. He said he wanted my mother to feel welcomed when she moved. Looking back, I think he was withholding feelings from me. I wonder now if those unexpressed feelings about mother and unspoken fears about what was happening to him physically caused him to turn to alcohol.

That spring, in response to a challenge from the stewardship committee to raise funds for the church, Hugh approached me to host a gourmet dinner. He sold four places. As was his style, he put out his finest china and silver, created a beautiful centerpiece, and served two couples from the Union Church an elegant meal. Afterwards, one of the couples reported that the food had been delicious but, in their opinion, Hugh had consumed too much wine. When I asked Hugh about the evening, he said, "Everybody had a good time."

In May 1981, on our last tour of the Holy Land with parishioners, Hugh took photographs for us but not for the group.

"I need a drink before we go out and face the natives," he would say.

He drank scotch or vodka in the hotel lounges. Once he walked out of one with the glass in his hand. Often, when Hugh and I joined the group, Hugh acted silly and his comments didn't add up. He frequently complained of indigestion and heartburn. I was disturbed by his behavior and concerned about his image with the other tour members. His unpredictable behavior created enormous anxiety on that trip, and I was glad to get home. I remember thinking I should monitor his drinking.

Moving Mother

Two weeks after we had returned from the Bibleland tour, Hugh and I rented a U-Haul van and drove to Williamsburg. I warned him that there would be no drinking on this trip. He agreed.

"Mother is still packing," my brother, Harold, said when we arrived. "She didn't give us much notice."

"I hope you know what you are doing Bob," his wife Jane said. "Your mother will be expecting her meals served on time."

"She'll have to wait until I can get it ready," I said. "What else should I expect?"

"She refuses to compromise when it comes to the television: she watches only her TV programs."

"Anything else?"

"She stays in the bathroom for a long time."

"I have plenty of bathrooms."

"She can be very demanding," Harold said.

"What do you mean?" I asked.

"Because she can pay her own expenses, she expects to be in charge," Harold said. "She means well, but over time her demands begin to grate on you. She's hard to please. Jane has been wonderful to her all these years, as good as she is with her own mother. But Mother just sort of expects it. You'll find out."

Once the van was loaded, Hugh placed a wooden step he had made on the ground in front of the van door. Holding her hand, he helped Mother into the van and steadied her as she sat down in her La-Z-Boy held in place between the two seats. Then he handed her two battery-operated fans to keep herself cool.

As I was backing out of the driveway, Mother said, "You're like your father, Bob. Remember what a good packer he was?"

After ten minutes of quiet riding, Mother said, "I don't want to be a burden to either one of you."

She repeated that phrase ten times before we reached Maynard.

Retirement

As Mother settled in, she demanded a schedule for her meals. She wanted to know when I would serve lunch and dinner. Knowing a fixed time gave her something to look forward to, to plan her schedule. We played one or two games of Scrabble every night. I enjoyed her company, although there were times that I felt tired and would have preferred not to cook. And there were other constraints, most having to do with ease in relating to Hugh. I couldn't just call him.

When I came home from work, Mother greeted me with suggestions: "The windows need washing," "the grass is getting kind of high, don't you think?" "You should wash the car before driving it to church on Sunday." "Your hair is getting a little long, don't you think?"

"Are you going to go out of the house looking like that?" Mother would say when I wore jeans to visit Hugh.

"Like what?" I replied. "Hugh likes the way I look."

"I'm just trying to be helpful," she would say.

And I would change my clothes.

"That's better," she would say.

Naturally, Hugh was disappointed when I arrived. He missed my jeans and leather. He felt me giving in to her. That problem was easy to resolve; I left a pair of jeans at Hugh's.

Looking back, I can see that I was trying to please everyone. I'm sure my heart was in the right place: I wished to make the people I cared most about happy. The sad result, I see now, was a constant internal struggle. And by allowing Mother to get away with rude behavior, I encouraged such behavior.

For the longest time, Mother made excuses not to accompany me to Hugh's for dinner. A whim, curiosity, or my obvious hurt at her refusal caused her to agree to go one day. Hugh had dinner waiting for us.

"Your table setting is lovely," she said.

"Thank you," Hugh said.

"Everything is delicious."

"Thanks."

"Who's that lady?" she asked, pointing at a painting.

"That's my mother," Hugh said, "I painted it years ago."

"I like it," Mother said.

On the way home, I said, "Now you know how homosexuals live."

"I don't like the word homosexual," Mother said. "I don't think it is a nice word for a minister to use. It has too much sex in it."

"But Mother, you're a heterosexual."

She looked offended.

"Hugh's mother was such a lovely looking lady," she said. "But his bold facial features and gaunt frame remind me of a scarecrow, and in those pants, he looks like one. If you two must be a couple, why couldn't he be better looking? He looks common in those jeans."

"He's good looking to me, Mother."

"He's not a good housekeeper either, he's messy. I doubt if his kitchen floor has been scrubbed recently. Did you see all those spots by the sink and stove?"

"I hadn't noticed," I said.

"And I can't stand the smell of his cigarette smoke. He's going to kill himself if he doesn't quit smoking. Since your father died, cigarette smoke really bothers me. Thank goodness you never started, Bobby."

"I'll try to get him to cut down."

I loved Mother very much, but I resented her feelings about Hugh and me. She had grown up in a previous era, I rationalized. She just couldn't understand. Perhaps she was jealous.

Over time, the circulation in Mother's legs worsened, so she spent most of her time with her feet up on a stool. She used a walker to move from her chair to the bathroom to bed and to the car. However, she preferred a cane when going to church, the beauty parlor, or shopping. Hugh was very good about helping her up the church steps on those Sundays she rode over in his car.

During the week I walked with her, helped her shop for clothes, do her banking, and post mail. I made sure she was safely in bed each night. I constantly worried about her falling.

I worried about Hugh, too. In the early eighties, friends in New York began to die of AIDS. Jack Challener died first, then Hans van der Molen, and Eddie Buchanan. We hadn't seen them for a while, but their passing, and the devastating effects of AIDS on the gay community, saddened us.

Hugh was also sad because he was not selling many paintings.

Then he had another stroke on his left side and lost the peripheral vision in his left eye. Again, he underwent physical therapy, most of which I heard about over the phone. Although he seldom asked for help, I felt guilty that I could not be with him every day to help him recover.

Again, he recovered strength in his left arm and leg, but previously undetected damage to interior muscles and nerves prolonged the healing process. To paint he had to move his eyes around the canvas to see what he was painting. Since he couldn't see to make left turns, he drove less and less.

One day, while Hugh was recuperating, a parishioner called the church office to tell me she had tried to call Mother, but she had not answered. Since Mother had made no plans to be away, I rushed home and found her lying in the kitchen floor. She hadn't detected swelling, and she was not in a lot of pain. She thought she could get up with my help. I insisted she get x-rays, which showed her aches and pains were bruises and strains. As she mended, I cooked and cleaned. I didn't visit Hugh for several weeks.

Upon my arrival the following week, I learned Hugh's telephone had been disconnected: he hadn't paid his bill. When I checked, I discovered other overdue bills. Looking over his check accounting, I noticed he had failed to deduct ATM withdrawals. I spent an entire day sorting out his finances and then took him out to eat at a local family restaurant.

The waitress there had seen us together over the years, and I assumed had surmised our relationship, so she didn't know what to think when Hugh started flirting with her.

"I'm trying to make my lover jealous," he said. "Bob, here, doesn't like women but I do."

I was hurt and embarrassed, and felt my efforts were not appreciated. I didn't seem to be able to please Hugh or my mother. Yet by trying to care for them, my pastoral work and administrative duties at church were being neglected. No one from the church complained, but I felt the pressure of not having enough time to prepare sermons adequately or make all the required visits. Something had to give, so when I saw an ad for Havenwood Heritage Heights, a retirement community in Concord, New Hampshire, I sent for a brochure.

Hugh visited the campus with me. We toured an enclave of one-bedroom cottages and studio apartments built on a beautiful campus of large pine trees interlaced in spring with wondrous pink lady slippers. I was surprised to learn that no two-bedroom options existed (they do now). Residents were out preparing the soil for flower gardens and tomato plants. The sidewalks connecting other blocks of cottages eventually led to a large health facility. I thought, if Mother and I took one of the cottages and she became disabled, she could go to the campus health facility. At that time, Hugh could come to live with me. I requested a place on the waiting list and resigned at church.

On April 30, 1986, one member from the Spring Valley church and three members from the Newark church came to Maynard to take part in my retirement service. Hugh, Mother, Kay, and PJ also came. One of the speakers said that during thirty-five years as a pastor, I preached 1,610 sermons and never missed a Sunday due to illness. Another speaker mentioned that I would have more time to spend with Hugh. The Maynard church gave me a bathrobe (Mother's suggestion to the committee), a large card from the Sunday school children, books, money, and a photo frame with fifteen photos—images from my travels, ministries, and interests. Maynard's selectmen declared April 27, 1986, as Rev. Robert Wood Day, and I felt honored.

Slipped on a Pea

In May 1986, Mother and I moved from Maynard to a one-bedroom cottage at Havenwood-Heritage Heights in Concord, New Hampshire.

Now ninety-one years old, Mother was fragile. She seemed lonely and a little depressed. Her legs and back ached constantly. She dressed herself. She read the *Boston Globe* and we played Scrabble and card games. We discussed what she might like for lunch and dinner, and I bought the groceries and fixed the meals. She usually washed the dishes and kept the stove and refrigerator clean and maintained a list of household items we needed. We took walks on the campus, sometimes stopping in at a neighbor's or sitting on one of the outdoor benches to chat with friends. I drove her to the doctor's office, dentist, and beauty parlor.

The Immanuel Congregation Church was a few blocks away. We attended Sunday worship there. Being a parishioner, participating in worship rather than having to lead it, was new and enjoyable. When I was asked to fill in for a visiting pastor, I always accepted.

Hugh had stopped going to church and rarely visited me in Concord. Impaired sight made him cautious about driving the thirty-five miles. Besides, there was not enough room in our apartment for him to stay overnight. On special occasions, like Christmas or Easter, I drove to Pepperell so he could be with us in Concord. He would spend the afternoon with Mother and me, and sleep at the Holiday Inn. Once guest cottages were developed at Havenwood, he stayed there.

When I talked to Hugh on the telephone, I could hear his sadness, his vitality diminishing.

Hugh's life, I could see, was deteriorating. His refrigerator usually contained stale food, which I threw away. As he was unable to push the vacuum, his rugs began to look dirty, so I vacuumed for him. I swept and mopped his kitchen floor and dusted his furniture. I cleaned his bathroom and changed the sheets on his bed, and gathered his dirty clothes scattered throughout the bedroom and washed them. Sometimes unchanged for days, the litter box smelled. His ashtrays were full of cigarette butts, and the house was filled with the stale smell of cigarette smoke. His garden, once well-tended, had become overgrown. Now and then, one could make out a blurred perennial blossom among the weeds. His screened-in porch and workbench were cluttered. He complained about not being able to find his tools. Since he worked in his studio less and less, more and more of his paintings were left unfinished. Seeing his circumstances caused my heart to ache.

"Why don't you come to live at Havenwood?" I'd say.

"What will I do with all my stuff?" he'd reply.

Once I visited and he said, "Let's rent a booth in a group antiques shop. Let's get rid of things we don't need or use. It will make it easier for you after I'm gone."

"Don't talk like that," I said.

"Why not?" he said. "It's the truth."

We rented a booth in an antiques shop we had frequently visited in West Townsend. Hugh sold his cut glass punch bowl set, andirons, an early automobile hood ornament, and a collection of his father's chauffeur badges.

He gave away his phonograph records, leather working tools, and Tiffany belt buckles. When I asked why, he said, "This way I know they will have a good home," he said.

"Look what I started," he said one day, leading me to the front bedroom of the house. There, outlined on a slanting wall, was a mural.

"What is it?" I asked.

"The first country we visited together?"

"Greece?"

"Yes," he said. "I like the Greeks—their food, history, the Parthenon, Acropolis, and the Athens Museum of Fine Arts."

"That's a great idea," I said. I was so glad to see him paint. For months the mural remained half-completed.

"When are you going to finish it?" I would ask.

"I'm leaving it unfinished, like my life," he said.

On my visits, instead of passionate lovemaking, we spent time cuddling, touching, kissing, and sharing endearing words.

We ate out a lot. I preferred meals at Denny's where the food was good and inexpensive, where they didn't serve drinks. But we usually ended up in a Chinese restaurant, where Hugh ordered a cocktail or two. Hugh preferred restaurants that served liquor. He knew I had lost a lung in the war but insisted on seats in the smoking section in restaurants. He lacked empathy; he seldom asked me how I felt. I blamed it on the drinking.

My love transcended any of Hugh's shortcomings; he was so perfect in every other way, and God knows what shortcomings Hugh endured with me.

Although much of the work of cleaning, washing clothes, and sorting through bills was unfinished, I would have to leave. Both of us waved goodbye as long as we could see each other, and I would always give a final honk on the horn as I drove out of sight.

I imagined Hugh, alone, listening to his classical music, fixing his supper, brewing a fresh pot of coffee, feeding his cat, leaving the dishes in the sink, watching TV or reading an art book, and smoking. I always felt guilty when I left him.

In January 1988, Hugh called early one morning.

"Bob, I've slipped on a pea," he said. "I didn't want you driving in the dark, so I waited to call. I haven't been able to get off the floor, but I've been crawling around. I found a pan under the sink to use as a toilet, and I pulled down the telephone to call you. But I'm getting thirsty, Bob, and I can't reach the faucet."

"Is the screen door locked from the inside?"

"Yes."

"Do you think you can reach it?"

"Yes."

"I'm on my way. Remember, I love you, and try not to worry, we've been through this before."

Anxiety and alarm filled my body. Slipped on a pea? I couldn't believe it.

I found him in the front room. He had managed to pull a pillow and a small blanket off the couch to put under his left hip and around his shoulders. He was crying when I came in. I knelt beside him and held him.

"I suppose we're going to that hospital, again?"

"Do you think you've had another stroke?"

"No. I told you. I slipped on a pea," he said. "My hip hurts bad."

"I'm going to call 911," I said. "Something might be broken. Just wait."

The ambulance arrived and I followed behind in my car.

Hugh's personal doctor insisted I wait in the waiting room with all my questions.

"We're going to put Mr. Coulter's left leg in traction," he told me after a long wait in the waiting room. "He'll have to be detoxed before we can operate. He was drunk and lost his balance."

Hugh remained in traction for three days prior to a hip socket replacement. When he finally came home, he was glad to see the cat and all his things. He could smoke and drink again. He could use the telephone. PJ and Kay dropped by more often. Seven and a half weeks of rehabilitation followed, with me constantly on the road between Concord and Pepperell. By March, he could walk with a four-footed cane. Using his cane, he would shuffle out to his studio, but he couldn't paint and hold on to the cane at the same time.

He drank. PJ told me that one of his friends would come by when I was not there and bring him liquor and stay and drink. I called Alcoholics Anonymous and requested a volunteer call on Hugh. Someone came twice, to no avail.

Again, I encouraged him to take a studio apartment at Havenwood, and he agreed to start the process.

"Maybe Edith will be in the Health Care Unit before a studio is available," he said, "Then I can move in with you."

I mentioned the idea of Hugh's move to Mother.

"If Hugh moves up here, I'll never get to see you," she replied.

Mr. Coulter's Pastor

In August, we took our twenty-fourth consecutive vacation to Ogunquit, Maine. We stayed in our usual place, the Old Village Inn, room four, which required walking two flights up. It took a long time for Hugh to climb the stairs with his cane. He kept one hand on the railing. People coming down the stairs stood back to give him room.

"I slipped on a pea and broke my hip," he'd say, and I'd feel angry.

Out on the street, instead of walking we waited for the trolley, and strangers offered Hugh their seats. We rode past the Ogunquit Art Museum—where each year previously, we stopped to see paintings on our way to Perkins Cove with its beautiful, rugged coastline. We tried to walk the Marginal Way, the walkway along the cliffs overlooking the sea. We walked about fifty yards, and then sat on a bench, watching the ocean and holding hands. Hugh, with his camera around his neck, wanted to take my picture sitting alone on the bench with the ocean behind me. I looked over the back of the bench, and Hugh snapped the picture.

At night we went to the Front Porch, a piano bar up another long flight of stairs. Hugh sat near the piano.

"What'll you have?" a cocktail waiter asked.

"Scotch on the rocks," Hugh said.

"Coke," I said.

Men around the piano sang Broadway tunes. Hugh joined them.

"That takes me back to Manhattan days," he said.

"Me too."

Young men stood around the bar. We checked out the young men, compared which ones we thought were sexy, and greeted men we had met in previous years.

After his second drink, I said, "Don't you think you ought to pace yourself?"

"These glasses are small," he said.

I warned him again after his third one.

"It wasn't a full glass," he said, and ordered another.

Going down the stairs after drinking was treacherous.

As we walked toward the Inn, we sat on a park bench, ate ice cream, and watched the crowd go by.

"Look at that bleached blond in the fish net top showing off his tan," I said.

"Too young," Hugh responded. "All looks and no experience."

"But I thought you liked blonds?"

"I did twenty-six years ago, but now I like gray."

"These men are getting younger and younger," I said.

"I think we're getting older and older."

"Let's call it a night."

In past years we had been out every day, walking on the beach or shopping. But that year, Hugh sat in the room, dreading the stairs. When we were ready to leave for home, Hugh told the Inn cashier, "See you next year without this damn cane."

In early December we put up our tree and wrote our Christmas letter. During the weekend, I discovered that one of Hugh's credit card companies had cancelled his card.

"Who needs a credit card where I am going?" he said.

Statements like that were hard to hear.

"You're getting better and better. It's just taking longer this time."

"I don't think so."

We sat quietly together, eating.

"I'm tired," he said. "I'm losing weight."

"Maybe you should eat more and smoke less," I said.

"I'm not going to do my income tax this year. They can't put a dead man in jail."

"Enough of that, dear. I know this has been a rough year for you, but the worst is over. I expect to have another twenty-six years with you before we cash in our chips."

On New Year's Eve, I drove to Pepperell to welcome in the New Year with Hugh. PJ joined us for dinner at a Chinese restaurant and to see the movie *Working Girl*. Afterwards, Hugh and I watched the ball drop in Times Square and toasted the New Year of 1989.

New Year's Day was on Sunday. We got up late. I attended church in nearby Townsend, while Hugh cooked. We had dinner around one o'clock. PJ came by. We were watching the Rose Bowl parade. I heard him tell PJ how he was losing weight. His fingers had gotten so thin that he carried his wedding ring in his jeans pocket.

Monday was a holiday. We were relaxed. I was trying to tidy up, get the laundry going, and check through his correspondence. There were several unopened letters.

I cleaned the bathroom.

Hugh took a bath.

We talked about things to sell at the antiques shop.

Hugh stayed up late; he said he wanted to "make a painting." He picked up an eighteen-inch square canvas and his charcoal, sat in his chair, and began to sketch. I gave him a fresh cup of coffee and his cigarettes. I fed the cat.

"Don't be too long," I said. "You don't have to finish it all in one night. I have to leave in the morning."

"I know," he said. We embraced each other.

"I'll be waiting for you." Hugh was watching an opera on television when I went to bed, and I didn't hear him come to bed. I got up early the next morning and emptied the ashtrays and made breakfast—a fresh pot of coffee and oatmeal.

"Hugh," I called up to him. "Breakfast is ready."

I pushed down the toast. Hugh didn't answer. I didn't hear his cane on the floor or the water running. I went to wake him.

When I entered our bedroom, Hugh was motionless, no sign of breathing. Our cat lay beside him. The covers were pulled up to Hugh's neck. He was on his back. The blanket was smooth. He looked peaceful. Light came in from the window. His face looked a little ashen, and his eyes were closed. Although Hugh's body was still warm from our white electric blanket, I could tell he was dead. I just knew.

I shook him. The cat jumped off the bed. Nothing. My insides fell out and I started to cry. I wondered what I should do. What happens now? He's dead, I thought. He was limp. I have to do something. Dial 911. I need help here.

I found his wedding ring and put it in my pocket. He had taken it out of his jeans, along with his change, and put it on a table beside our bed. I picked up the telephone. I thought about the onslaught of emergency vehicles and police. These were my last moments alone with Hugh. I put the receiver down.

Kneeling beside the bed, I prayed a prayer of gratitude for our life together. Tears rolled down my face. Then I dialed 911.

A police car arrived followed by an ambulance. I went out on the porch. The policeman came up on the porch.

"Who are you?" he asked. His question took me by surprise. I felt intimidated.

"Rev. Robert Wood," I replied. "Hugh's been ill, and I've been checking in on him from time to time.

"Where's the body?" the policeman asked as the ambulance assistants came up the stairs. They followed me upstairs to the bedroom. I stood back. One ambulance assistant felt Hugh's pulse and agreed that he was dead.

The policeman looked out the window to check the roof. He looked in the hallway then came back into the bedroom and asked, "Was there anybody else in the house?"

"No. Just the two of us."

"When did you discover the body?"

"About twenty minutes ago."

The ambulance assistance asked, "Who is his doctor?"

I told him.

"His name?" he asked, speaking of Hugh.

"Hugh Macmaster Coulter."

"Address?"

I told him.

"Age?"

"69."

"And what is the nature of your relationship?"

I wanted to tell him that Hugh was my spouse, the love of my life, my mate, my partner in life, my lover, the one that had given so much romance and meaning to my life, but I uttered simply, "I'm Mr. Coulter's pastor."

They filled out a death certificate.

Hugh's doctor lived a block away. He came right away, felt for Hugh's pulse, and listened through his stethoscope. Cause of death, he determined, was heart failure.

"Any signs of foul play?" asked the policeman.

"He's been ill," I said.

Then they all left. Hugh's body was still upstairs. I called a United Church of Christ minister in Townsend, a Reverend Neal Lund. Rev. Lund came right over.

Pastor Lund stayed with me while the body was taken out.

Shaking, through tears, I said, "You realize that Hugh was my lover."

Rev. Lund put his arm around me and said, "Yes, I know. I appreciate the reality that you have lost the most important person in your life." I cried.

"Would you be willing to conduct a memorial service at your church in Townsend? Feel free to say no. I don't want to embarrass you with your congregation or deacons."

"No problem," he said.

Soon I was alone in an empty house. The end, I thought. What am I going to do now? I cried. It was the first time I had been in that house alone. I felt lost and lonely.

I discovered the canvas Hugh had started on which were drawn with six charcoal lines in various shapes, circles with slashes. It suggested expansion, openness. I cried for a long time.

Late that evening, when I finally returned to Havenwood much later than planned, Mother said, "Why are you so late?"

"Hugh died," I said, as I sat in a chair, with my head buried in my hands. I kissed the ring on my left hand, and, remembering that I had put Hugh's in my pocket, took it out to kiss. I began to cry, shaking, confused, feeling overwhelmed by grief.

"Why couldn't it have been me?" she said.

Mother was ninety-three years old. She could no longer bathe herself and frequently forgot to take her medication. I couldn't feel anger towards her.

Grief

During the weeks that followed, letters of sympathy arrived from New Hampshire Conference Staff as well as at least a dozen of my parishioners from all three of my previous parishes. Having spent so many years concealing the nature of my relationship with Hugh, I was surprised and touched by such a show of concern. They probably knew more about us than I realized.

Having heard the news of Hugh's passing from Mother, my brother and his wife sent a condolence card, with a promise to send a contribution to the Maynard Church in Hugh's memory. They didn't call, which disappointed me. I felt they didn't understand my loss. Although they had met Hugh only a few times, I hoped Mother might have talked to them about us.

The day before the service, I stopped at a floral shop in Pepperell, where Hugh stopped regularly on the way to pick up his mail. He'd say to the florist, "How many flowers can I get for a dollar today?" And the florist would offer him a bouquet of day-old flowers.

"Can I help you?" a woman said from behind the counter.

"Do you remember Hugh Coulter?" I asked.

"Yes, I was sorry to hear that he had passed away."

"His memorial service is tomorrow. Instead of a typical funeral bouquet, I would like to order a sculptured arrangement, an original sculpture of flowers."

She showed me a piece of driftwood. "Maybe I can design something around this."

After I left her shop, I realized I had never bought Hugh flowers before and felt guilty. A list began to grow in my head of all the things I had not been able to do for him. Time popped up over and over: I hadn't given him enough time.

January 21 was a cold but sunny day; a day Hugh would have loved because of the contrasts between a deep blue sky with billowing clouds and deep green firs and pines.

I wore a gray suit for parishioners and boots for Hugh.

"God, help me get through the day," I prayed. "Hold me in your loving arms. Keep me from breaking down."

I drove to the Pepperell house. PJ and Kay were there, preparing food to receive people after the service. They had cleaned up the house, and had used Hugh's good linen, china, and silver to set a table. I was so grateful for their help.

I picked out six of Hugh's painting along with four of his enlarged photographs of Bibleland scenes. Hugh's life was in his work, I thought.

Through waves of sadness and tears, I drove alone to the Congregational Church in Townsend. I wanted to arrive first to make sure everything was in order. The organist, also early, saw me struggling to group the paintings and photographs on the chancel. We searched a back room and found boxes against which I could lean Hugh's work.

As soon as the chancel was settled, the florist arrived with her arrangement—driftwood mounted in stones surrounded by green ferns and flowers. Hugh would have loved the bouquet's natural feeling and the explosion of color, I thought. I placed the flowers on a table in front of the pulpit.

The organist began to play, "Jesu Joy of Man's Desiring." Other floral bouquets appeared. People began to take their seats in the pews. I looked for people I knew and saw only one gay man (a friend of PJ's), a female artist from Townsend, two carloads from the Maynard Church, a few neighbors from around the Pepperell house, the owners of the antiques shop in West Townsend, PJ and Kay.

The sanctuary, oddly shaped like a wedge, bigger in the back, sounded empty and hollow except for intermittent coughing. I sat alone on the short front pew. Just before Rev. Lund began his remarks, PJ and Kay sat on either side of me. Their caring touched me.

The music stopped and Rev. Lund stood up to speak. He talked about God's healing love, grief, anger, and emptiness.

He read Scripture verses that I had suggested: Psalm 48, Psalm 122, the words of The Last Supper, the story of Golgotha, and Acts 1:6–12, descriptive of places Hugh and I had visited in our travels.

Rev. Lund's words were like old friends: I had used them many times to help others in their time of need. Now, the words, tried and true, were sharing this hour of grief with me. He prayed another comforting prayer, and we sang "Blessed Be the Tie That Binds." After the benediction, PJ and Kay left immediately for Pepperell. I stood, broken-hearted, in the aisle. People came up to me to shake my hand and embrace me. Viola

Merriam and her husband, Herb, parishioners from Maynard, stood patiently waiting their turn to speak to me. Viola said, "I'm sorry you lost your friend Bob," as she gave me a hug.

"He was more than my friend; he was my lover!" I shouted, without a thought to who heard.

"Well, you know, he's not dead, he's with God."

"Yes, that's our faith," I said. I cried again.

Viola gave me another hug while the others waited. One of Hugh's artist friends from Pepperell lingered. I sensed she was waiting to be alone with me.

Finally, she came up and embraced me.

"I think Hugh would have been pleased by this service," she said. "It was a nice thing for you to do. What a nice touch that you had his paintings. You must have had a good relationship."

"We did," I said.

Three days after Hugh's memorial service, I drove to the Townsend Funeral Parlor to pick up a heavy cardboard box containing Hugh's ashes. I carried them back to Havenwood and placed them on a shelf in a big walk-in closet.

Mother saw the box as I came in the front door.

"What are you going to do with that?" she asked. "Are you going to buy a cemetery plot?"

"Hugh had asked me to pour his ashes into the Aegean Sea," I said.

"Oh," she said. "When will you be doing that?" I think she was worried that I would be away.

"I have no plans yet. There's no hurry. Later this year, maybe."

Grace

Six months after Hugh died, a nurse quietly said to me, "I think it is time for your mother to move to the healthcare unit."

"So that time has come," was my mother's simple response.

She was quite noble about the move. She knew it would make life easier for me and ease my worry about leaving her alone.

I visited her three times a day. After breakfast I took the *Boston Globe* that I had read to her. After lunch I picked up and delivered her mail. After dinner I showed up for a game of Scrabble.

If she needed shoes for winter or a spring coat, a different scarf or a handbag, I gladly took them to her. I helped her manage her affairs, pay her bills, and balance her checkbook. Each Sunday, I wheeled her to the afternoon Vespers service in the dining room. Sometimes, we took rides in the country or ate out. When we were not together, I took comfort knowing she received the care she needed that I couldn't provide.

Now alone, I had plenty of time to think about Hugh. Each time I heard a song we shared together, I cried. And I cried, driving to Pepperell to sort through his estate, most of which he left to me.

On the table beside his bed, I found the gold chain Hugh wore until his death. I visualized Hugh's face and neck adorned by the chain and his image was so real I could almost touch it. Also, on the table were two five-by-seven photographs Hugh had taken of me, images of me he had looked at all those years we had lived apart. I brought those three items home with me after the first day of sorting.

Another day, I brought home a golden Chinese urn, Hugh's stickpin collection, his leathers, thousands of photographs and slides, cameras, and jewelry including six crosses he made. On other days, I made room for Hugh's family photographs, his childhood Sunday school attendance pins, a lock of his mother's hair, his ruby thumb print glass collection, his canary Sandwich candlestick, a four-tier-center-post table, a seventeenth-century English oak armchair, all his paintings (fifty of them), and boxes filled with small things. I consoled myself, thinking I am keeping the very best, like his favorite possession: two small, yellow bronze bird inkwells. All these items held a new significance for me as physical reminders of Hugh's time on the earth.

I couldn't keep everything. I filled dozens of garbage bags with cancelled checks, photos I couldn't identify, old files from his work, used tubes of paint, and old brushes: I felt I was tossing out bits of his life. Antiques dealers came for larger items.

After all that sorting, selling, and donating, I was emotionally drained, sad, and empty. I felt there was no one with whom I could share my grief. I felt increasingly lonely, increasingly aware of my isolation. Few people knew of our love for each other, our wedding, or our commitment to each other through the years.

I began to second guess our decision to live apart and recalled moments when we had changed our conversations or stopped an impulse to hold hands or kiss so as not to offend people, protecting others from our being gay. I couldn't hold Hugh's hand now. I couldn't kiss him or hug him.

Homophobia—fear or antipathy towards gays, lesbians, bisexuals, and transgender persons—was being discussed a lot in those days. I recalled my dislike for the effeminate gays at Oberlin. I wondered if I was homophobic, if my internalized homophobia caused me to treat Hugh with less respect than I would have if I had been married to a woman. Would I have allowed my mother to move in with me? Shouldn't I have insisted that Hugh be with me at Havenwood? These questions haunted me as well as thoughts of time lost. Gone were the moments Hugh and I could have been together in the evenings after work, lying next to each other throughout the night and cuddling in the morning.

I found myself blaming the Church for those missed opportunities and felt anger towards an institution that was supposed to embody love and acceptance in which I felt the need to deny myself, to hide. As much as I wanted to place blame on external factors, I also understood that I needed to see my part in it.

Reading Scripture helped, particularly 1 John 4:18: "There is no fear in love, but perfect love casts out fear; for fear has to do with punishment, and whoever fears has not reached perfection in love."

I meditated on fear, the fear that surrounded my life—parental expectations, military rules and regulations, the qualifications for ordination, McCarthyism, and bigotry. I recalled how I dreaded church meetings, fearing someone might discover our secret and I'd be fired. The love of Christ had been available to me, but I chose fear. I had been less than I wanted to be. I had not been honest. I had not loved, fully, so I was left with this consequence of regret.

I confessed through prayers, asking God's forgiveness. Confession could not undo my acts or decisions, but I became less bound up by them. Confession could not bring Hugh back either, but it lessened the guilt I felt for all I hadn't been able to do for him and prepared me to fulfill Hugh's request to have his ashes scattered in the Aegean Sea.

In September 1990, in response to an ad I saw in *The Advocate*, I signed up for a gay tour of Greece organized by Hanns Ebenstein. Midway through the tour, seven men, all strangers—a funeral director, a doctor, an architect, a hairdresser, a chief of police—Hanns, and myself boarded a fishing boat leaving from Mykonos to Delos. During the boat ride over, I explained my intention to cast Hugh's ashes in the sea.

On our return trip to Mykonos, while the boat swayed in choppy seas, I brought Hugh's ashes to the side of the boat, where all the men huddled around me.

"I've done a burial at sea if I can be of any help," the funeral director said.

"Thanks," I said and handed him the box.

He opened the box and lifted out a black plastic bag with half of Hugh's ashes. The rest would be buried with me.

"Do you want me to throw in the bag or just the ashes?"

"Just pour the ashes."

"Tell me when."

"About halfway."

"Shall I tell the captain to stop the boat?"

"That's not necessary."

Crying, I passed out three or four pictures of Hugh and me to show the other fellows what Hugh looked like. I tried to read a short liturgy of prayers and a committal-at-sea, but I couldn't read. I kept repeating the words, "Unto thee, O Lord, do we commit these earthly remains of our beloved Hugh Coulter unto Thy eternal care." The undertaker leaned over the side of the boat, looking at me. I nodded, and he poured out the ashes, which floated into the sea. I tossed the photographs overboard and watched them float on top of the water.

"Let's continue this in the cabin," someone said.

Inside, the six men embraced me. Some of them cried. I felt these strangers understood and sympathized with my pain more fully than people I knew for years, more fully than my living relatives.

Soon after returning from the trip, I attended my first National Gathering of the United Church Coalition for Lesbian/Gay Concerns, begun years before by Bill Johnson. I was the oldest man there. I knew only three of the eighty-five people in attendance. Several were seeking prayers, spiritual comfort, and direction to help them cope with AIDS. Leaders offered instructions on coming out of the closet.

I talked about my life with Hugh and his death. Again, strangers, having listened, sensing my sadness, hugged me when I cried. Several people tried to comfort me. The ministry for homosexuals I so earnestly sought through *Christ and the Homosexual* and my work with the Board for Homeland Ministries had taken the form of this gathering. Because of the ministries of others, UCC churches throughout the United States were engaged in education, discussion, and taking votes to become Open and Affirming.

At the closing banquet, I was presented with a certificate honoring me as "a Ground Breaker for the Coalition." Receiving affirmation for my attempts at advocacy pleased me. However, the lessons on coming out of the closet had more profound effect: I recognized that back home in my local parish, I remained closeted, as I had been during my entire career. I also recognized that my relatives needed to know about my life with Hugh. I had work to do.

In life, I was learning, we are as alive as we allow those we love to know us in our completeness: that which we conceal is dead already.

Blood

Mother died the following year, and Harold and Jane, my brother and his wife, came up for a memorial service I arranged at Havenwood.

After the service, the three of us went through Mother's things stored in my apartment. As we sorted through old clothes, photographs, and jewelry, Harold and Jane reminisced about Mother living with them, and I told stories of her time with me.

Harold and Jane took, as Mother had wished, Mother's diamond rings—one for Jane and one for their daughter, Pat—and some family photographs. Jane also took a few pieces of

Mother's costume jewelry and several handbags. They filled two boxes to ship to Virginia.

During our time together, they said nothing about Hugh's paintings, which hung on almost every wall, nor did they mention the photographs of him I kept prominently displayed. I wanted to say, "Aren't you the slightest bit curious?"

The next day I drove the three of us to Vermont, where we buried Mother's ashes in Father's grave. Harold hired a stonecutter to add Mother's name to our family memorial, an obelisk of granite, ten feet tall. After the service, I drove them to their friend's house and rode home alone, saddened that they hadn't spoken about Hugh and hadn't asked me how I might be coping with the loss. Perhaps they were grieving for Mother, but I resented their apparent insensitivity.

The following spring, they invited me to visit them at the Sunnyside Presbyterian Retirement Community in Harrisonburg, Virginia. Hoping to forge some sort of meaningful connection with them, I accepted their invitation.

Entering their house, I quickly left my bags in the den and joined Harold, who was eager for me to see their place. First stop, their front porch that overlooked a flower garden Jane had planted. Next, we toured the living room/dining area decorated with carved wooden furniture, a cuckoo clock, a collection of steins, Hummel figurines, all bought when Harold had been stationed in Germany. We sat in the living room for several hours, reminiscing while looking at photos of their vacations and children.

The next morning, Jane took me to the healthcare unit to meet some of her patients who were mostly bedridden and frail. Trained as a nurse's aide, Jane volunteered her services there. Her patients seemed pleased to see her. She introduced me as her brother-in-law, Rev. Robert Wood, and I prayed with a few of them.

That afternoon, Harold and Jane took me to see a Civil War Museum. They both knew a great deal about Confederate generals, Civil War battle flags, and the sequence of battles, and I enjoyed learning the history.

Later that day, while Jane cooked dinner, Harold showed me his office. As I looked over Civil War books and maps, pictures of General Robert E. Lee, and military decorations, Harold pulled out a handgun from his desk.

"This is for protection if we need it," he said, "and I've taught Jane how to handle it."

I was shocked to see it. We hadn't been raised with guns in our home. Our father would have been appalled. I didn't touch it.

Harold offered me a cocktail. I declined.

On Sunday, they took me to church.

"This is my brother, the minister," Harold told his Sunday school class.

He seemed proud. Everyone I met there was cordial. After church, I invited Harold and Jane out for Sunday dinner.

At the dinner table our conversations floated between family matters (their children) and politics.

"Hillary Clinton seems to be running her husband and the country," Harold said at one point. "But maybe she would do a better job than that draft dodger of a husband of hers. He'd better not try to get more gays in the armed forces."

How I had wanted to tell him about the men with Q's on their backs and let him know that gay men could serve their country with honor. I felt my mouth open, but I just couldn't challenge him. I feared his rejection; he was my last living relative. Or maybe I couldn't challenge him because of lingering childhood feelings of inferiority and jealousy. I didn't want to give him anything to hang over me.

I left Virginia feeling less connected to Harold and Jane than before. To be with them, I thought, meant I would sit and listen to their stories about travel and children and his politics and thoughts on religion. But there was no equal time for me to talk about my life with Hugh and how much I missed him or my thoughts about how the church should be a place where everyone is welcomed at the table. I said to myself, I've had enough: I'll write and end our relationship before he does.

I wrote Harold and Jane a letter to thank them for their hospitality and announced that I probably wouldn't be coming to visit them anymore.

Yet, cards from them continued to arrive at Christmas, Thanksgiving, Valentine's Day, Halloween, and on my birthday. Inside the cards were letters describing their most recent activities in church, the United Daughters of the Confederacy, the Country Club, and news about their children, vacations, movies they had seen, and health problems. Sometimes they sent gifts.

In one of their cards, Jane wrote that Harold had been in an automobile accident and was more "shook up than hurt." I prayed prayers of thanksgiving that he had been spared serious injury and asked God to be present in his healing. Perhaps thoughts of how fragile life is and my prayers for him caused me to reach out again. I had to talk to him, I thought. If I'm ever going to have a meaningful relationship with him, I must tell him about myself. I sat in my living room, trembling, with the telephone receiver in my hand.

Harold answered. His cordial, pleasant greeting seemed to indicate he was pleased to hear my voice.

"Harold, I'm just calling to see how you are feeling after the accident?"

"I'm still sore," he said, "but feeling lucky to be alive."

"Thank God," I said. "I've been praying for you."

"Thanks," he said.

"I've been doing a lot of thinking about my life with Hugh and my relationship with you, and I need to talk about it."

I told him that a rumor surfaced when I had been at the University of Pennsylvania about a man named Wood who had organized fraternity brothers to visit gay bars in Philadelphia to beat up gays—"homos," I guess, they were called then.

"Did you beat up homos in college?" I asked him.

"Lord no, I would never do anything like that."

I reminded him about my engagement to Helen after the war.

"I'm not sure if, or how much, my engagement might have fooled you, but, as we both know now, there would be no more girls in my life after Helen."

"I guess we were fooled. We had every reason to believe you wanted to marry Helen."

I told him about Fred Igler's letter to Oberlin Seminary.

"I thought my career was over before it had begun," I said.

"This is news to me. You must have been devastated."

"I was." I stopped talking for a moment, holding in my emotions. "You went back into the service to Fort Eustice and then on to Newfoundland. We stayed in touch, exchanging letters and photos. You wrote about your children, Jane, and your work, and I wrote about my ministry and news about Mother and Dad, unable to write about my struggle to find a lover. I remembered the military prohibition against homosexuality and assumed you wouldn't approve."

"I probably wouldn't have approved."

"Yet, I was hoping to change such negative attitudes towards homosexuals by writing *Christ and the Homosexual.* By sending you a copy of that book, I was trying, once more, to tell you about myself. But you never responded to that book. Did you read it? What did you think?"

"Sure, we read it a long time ago. I do remember not agreeing with some of your ideas, but I didn't conclude you were gay because of it."

"I guess the first time you met Hugh was when Dad died, just six weeks after Hugh and I had met. Of course, Dad died without knowing for sure that I was gay; or if he did, he didn't let on. He never mentioned anything to you, did he?"

"No."

"Hugh met you, me, and Mother at LaGuardia, and drove us to Spring Valley. Of course, we were filled with the emotions surrounding our father's passing, so there was no reason for you to notice anything."

"That's right."

"Later, Hugh and I privately exchanged wedding rings and vows, but we decided not to share the nature of our relationship with anyone except gay friends. I feared losing my job, and rejection, especially of family members."

"You probably would have lost your job."

"Through the years, we spent all our free time together. He traveled with me to visit Mother in Florida. We took vacations together. He joined my church. We were a couple in every sense of the word. Did you ever notice that I wore a ring?"

"No, I didn't."

"Did you notice any verbal references I might have made about an artist friend? Did Mother ever mention Hugh's visits?"

"Maybe so, but nothing that caught my attention."

"Did it ever occur to you that I might be gay?"

"Only recently."

"How about when we came to pick up Mother from your house in Williamsburg?"

"By that time, we had concluded what the situation was."

"After that, we continued to exchange letters, cards, and presents. You have always been polite. And as your children got older, and began to experience their difficulties, again, you shared your concerns with me. But I never felt like I could talk about Hugh's strokes or his struggle with alcohol or the pressures I felt being pulled between Mother, the church, and Hugh."

"That's too bad."

"Then Hugh died, and I wrote to tell you. Your condolence didn't seem to grasp my pain. In fact, because of your conservative politics and membership within the National Rifle Association, I had thought you might be anti-gay."

"You are correct about that. I am."

"I feel it. Maybe that is why I felt so uncomfortable when I visited you last. You did so many things to make me feel at home, but underneath all that was this feeling of disapproval to the point I had difficulty being myself. I felt like I had to censor myself. Of course, nothing would please me more than to find acceptance from my brother. You do understand that I am a gay man, don't you?"

"Yes."

"Does this fact bother you?"

"I'll be honest with you. Gay people bother me. I don't accept it as a normal lifestyle, but not as far as you are concerned: it is one thing to be against an issue, but Bob, you are blood. Jane and I both love you. I hope you know that."

Tears streamed down my face.

"I'm glad," I said. "We'll talk again soon. I'm glad you're okay."

"Good to hear from you," he said.

Harold could affirm some aspects of my life, it seemed, but not my gay life. That part of me, I assumed he was saying, remained a problem. I never sought his approval again.

A Witness

After Mother's death, I continued to attend the East Congregational United Church of Christ, a small church not far from the Havenwood Retirement Community. Many senior citizens from Havenwood went to church there.

I understood longstanding church members wouldn't know my abilities. I would attend church, the annual meetings, church suppers and coffee hours, and when opportunities for service presented themselves, I shared my skills. In time, I hoped, I might be nominated for various church committees.

I knew the pastor, Rev. Marilyn Bushnell, from my work on the AIDS Committee for the New Hampshire Conference.

Bushnell was a former nurse and very much concerned that churches be educated about the disease. At that time, AIDS was perceived to be a gay male problem, with death the outcome. At workshops throughout the state, our committee encouraged church folks to visit, pray for, and offer healing services for those sick with the disease. I came out easily to this group.

Bushnell was personally, privately supportive, but other than an occasional mention of those with AIDS in her pastoral prayer, her support was not articulated in the context of worship at church. I took her reluctance to pray for justice in the political struggle gays and lesbians faced to mean she was not ready to take a public stand. Privately, she warned me that such positions could be divisive.

One Sunday, when Rev. Bushnell asked me to supply preach for her, I preached about our need for heroes and heroines, those who inspire and challenge us to do more, who bring out the best in us, uphold genuine standards, and seem less concerned about themselves, choosing to accentuate the cause or causes they represent.

"I consider the members of this congregation to be heroes in the way you've welcomed me into your spiritual family," I said. "Five years ago, I came here as a stranger, and you made me welcomed."

Then I uttered the unspeakable through tears.

"Perhaps you've not been aware, but you've welcomed a gay man."

I expected rejection.

During the post-worship coffee hour, I experienced no overt hostility, embarrassment, or disappointment. In fact, some said positive words. A younger woman, who was a Sunday school teacher, embraced me.

"Thank you for sharing that. I'm proud of you," she said.

After Bushnell retired, I was asked to serve on the search committee that would meet many months before calling Rev.

Patricia Dubois to serve as our minister. When I told Dubois about myself, she let me know that she had a gay nephew and a lesbian friend. In worship, she regularly included gays, lesbians, bisexuals, and transgender Christians in her pastoral prayers. When appropriate she introduced articles she had read in *Waves*, the quarterly publication by the UCC Coalition for Lesbian, Gay, and Transgender Concerns. I felt more and more at home, until a Sunday that happened to fall on a Veteran's Day, an important day to me.

For me, Veteran's Day always presented an opportunity in worship to honor veteran members, and pray for Gold Star parents, MIAs, POWs, and those in VA hospitals. On such Sundays throughout my lifetime, I was accustomed and looked forward to seeing the names of those affected by war listed in the church bulletin, singing patriotic hymns, and seeing the American flag placed prominently in the sanctuary. Veterans from all wars should never be forgotten. Young men and women going to war should be remembered. After all, they put their lives on the line to protect our freedom.

When I attended East Church on Veterans Day, 2001, I immediately looked for such recognition in the church bulletin. Nothing. There were no patriotic hymns. Veterans weren't mentioned in the pastoral prayer or sermon. I thought maybe Dubois was waiting to include the recognition in her benediction. Nothing.

I left the service feeling unappreciated and let down. I wrote a letter to the moderator of the church council, expressing my feelings and demanding an explanation from the pastor. None came. I paid my pledge for 2001 and began to attend Vespers services at Havenwood. I no longer sought fellowship in a church.

Apples in the Tree of Life

As a retired United Church of Christ minister, I sense an uncharted course. You might think that by the time one becomes eight-three years old, there will be no uncharted courses left. But in recent years I feel that I have set out on one. It may be dark or filled with glorious light.

My beloved artist, rodeo cowboy Hugh perhaps prepares the way for my entry onto this uncharted course, but I will discover it alone. It will be my final course on earth. I detect my advance towards it through my body, health, faith, and environment.

My body has changed through the years. My hair has become white and thin. My once strong, muscular body has become weaker. It has more flesh drooping in folds. My skin has a different texture—taut and dry. The war wound in my chest is gradually choking me. I will be eating and swallowing, then suddenly the food refuses to go down like a stopped-up sink drain, plugged just behind the bullet hole scar. This internal wound involuntarily contracts like a vise around any seepage. It produces painful spasms. Food takes forever to get through. My body is not the same body that used to cruise up and down the beach at Provincetown in bikini swim trunks. Now, I keep it mostly covered up.

Here at Havenwood, our apartments are equipped with emergency cords which, when pulled, automatically unlock our front door and set off an alarm. Hearing an alarm bell is always cause for concern.

When my physical condition declines to a certain point, like my mother, I will be transferred from my apartment to a room in a building with full-time nursing care. That building sits in the middle of our campus, a constant reminder of our mortality.

There are thirty-four people living in thirty-two units on my block. We are widows, widowers, and couples. I am the only gay man in our block that I know of. We plan potluck suppers and summertime lawn parties where we celebrate birthdays, acknowledge those who have moved on to the nursing facility, and remember those who have passed away. We eat and talk mostly of health, travel, and family. We share memories. We look after each other. We all know the only exit out of here is the grave, so we try to make the best of it. We are realistic.

All I ask is strength to get through my daily tasks. I deliberately walk for exercise. Each morning, I walk to the Cumberland Farms store to get the *Boston Globe* and to the Havenwood office to pick up my mail, less than four blocks round trip. I walk up to four miles a day in nice weather.

Every other day I exercise in my living room—sets of push-ups, running in place, knee and leg raisers, with ten deep breaths in between. I diet. That's all I can do other than go for my annual physical, where I stand before my doctor who feels here and there, listens through a cold stethoscope, then reminds me about diet.

I still feel sexy and that pleases me. I get the old urges. They come when I have dreams about Hugh or when I see a sexy fellow on television or around town. I see them and feel attracted but keep it to myself. Or I read stories in *The Advocate* or go to a local bookstore that sells gay magazines.

Hugh's paintings cover my walls—lake scenes, roses, a green pepper, cucumbers, our Siamese cat, Meow, two schooners at Wiscasset, Maine, hanging plants held in jute, and many pure abstracts exploding with color and geometric images.

My favorite painting of Hugh's is a cowboy, which hangs over my bed. In 1959, three years before we met, still in his rodeo days, Hugh painted this self-portrait. In it he wears jeans, a hand-tooled leather belt with a buckle he designed, a cowboy hat, kerchief, and a cowboy shirt—the same gear he wears in the picture I keep of him by my telephone in the living room. He's riding a horse in the painting. His body is long and lean. His head is tilted as if seeking balance on the horse. One hand holds the reins, and the other is over his heart. His crotch presses against the pommel. Abstract colors in the background are like prisms of light pushing his figure forward. They create a sense of motion, of life, of sparkle. The obvious crotch bouncing on the saddle as the horse moves forward reminds me of our passionate love making the night we met and over the years. Sometimes Hugh comes to me in dreams. I miss him terribly, like a husband who had long been married to his wife would miss her when she had died, or a wife who had been long married would miss her deceased husband.

Hugh figures in almost every aspect of my surroundings. Hanging beside Hugh's paintings are his photographs of parishioners. One photograph captures a group from the Zion

United Church of Christ, Newark, New Jersey. The group was standing on Mount Zion in Palestine during one of our Bibleland tours. There are also small photographs of Hugh and me when we were younger.

Hugh's ring, which matches the ring I still wear on my finger, lies in front of these pictures. I can take one look at that gold circle and be immediately transported back to the night that we sat together in my parsonage and celebrated our commitment to each other with rings and vows. For a moment, I am overwhelmed with feelings of joy, and completeness. Then I remember again that Hugh is dead, and I cry and feel unfulfilled, incomplete, and old.

I know I'm not young anymore, nor do I worship the young. Why should I? My experience of many young people makes me feel dead already. Younger gay men, particularly, seem not to see me. I think they consider me a has-been who might have been interesting once but is pretty much out of the picture now.

In my opinion, I still have a life to live. I can be a help to the gay cause. I can be a help to my neighbors. I can still serve God. I teach a Lenten Bible series at Havenwood. I preach. I have some accumulated knowledge, experience, and memories.

Carl Jung once wrote:

> With increasing age, contemplation, and reflection, the inner images naturally play an ever-greater part in man's life. In old age one begins to let memories unroll before the mind's eye and, musing, to recognize oneself in the inner and outer images of the past. This is like preparation for an existence in the hereafter, just as, in Plato's view, philosophy is a preparation for death.

I try to see the line that leads through my life into the world, and out of the world again.

I confront my inner images, not with Plato's philosophy, but with a deep-rooted faith established from many years of reading

Scripture, prayer, and worship. My inner images are nurtured through beauty and mystery—in nature and the holiness of God's sanctuary; and by the sacraments—eating and drinking the symbols of the body and blood of Jesus.

I have worked hard to prepare for my final days, which are coming, which every person should prepare for. Before then, I sincerely hope to be at peace with God, the church, my world, my family, and Hugh. I realize now that my first step towards that end was coming out of the closet, which liberated me from fear.

Articles about *Christ and the Homosexual* have now been published in *The Advocate* and Boston's *Gay Community News*. *Out* magazine has included me among its photo essay of thirteen silent pioneers of the gay rights movement. Equality Forum has honored me as a pioneer for LGBTQ+ rights. I've participated in the Concord Interfaith Council Holocaust Service where I brought to remembrance the half million pink-triangle men martyred in that horror. I've served on the Conference Trustee's Committee, which encourages churches to think about LGBTQ+ issues as well as provide resources for serious study. I've appeared on local television to express my point of view on the subject of gays in the military. The congressman in my district invited me to Washington for a breakfast with President Bill Clinton. My picture has appeared on the front pages of local newspapers along with articles about my experience as a gay veteran. Neighbors here at Havenwood have clipped copies of the articles and taped my television appearances.

Several years ago, a newly formed Diversity Committee at Havenwood voted to change the word sexual "preference" to "orientation," affirming my experience. "In my life," I had told the committee, "there had been no choice to be or become a homosexual; rather, only a choice to be honest about it." Other gay couples have moved to Havenwood-Heritage Heights.

In 1993 I received an invitation to buy an apple on a "Tree of Life," a project to raise funds at Havenwood. An announcement was made in our weekly Havenwood–Heritage Heights paper. Jane Hurst, our Vice President for Development at the time, was in charge. I stopped by her office. She gave me a brochure.

Leaves, she explained, were the lowest price; apples, middle price; and building blocks at the base of the tree were the most expensive.

I could afford two apples. I thought it over and called Jane's office.

"If there are any apples left, put me down for two," I said.

I told Jane that I would write down what I wanted inscribed on my apples.

"In loving memory of Hugh M. Coulter, my spouse of twenty-six+ years. Rev. Robert W. Wood." For the other apple I wrote: "In loving memory of Jack * Hans * Ed, gay friends who died of AIDS. Rev. Robert W. Wood."

I took those three-by-five cards to Jane.

"Do you really want to use the word spouse?" she asked. "What about partner?"

"No, I prefer spouse because that means married. Partner doesn't necessarily mean married."

Jane thought for a minute.

"I guess that's right."

"But I don't want to get you into any hot water for my using the word *spouse*," I said.

"I'll check it with Bruce Edwards." He was the president of Havenwood.

"That's alright with me."

Several days later Jane called to say my apples were all set. Recently, I went to see them. The trunk is an actual carving of an older man, bald headed with a mustache, wearing glasses. The old man is wearing a sports shirt, which suggests to me a leisure life. His arm is extended so his hand rests upon a young woman's shoulder, his daughter I assume. Her arm is around her father's waist. The daughter's mother, wearing a dress, stands on the other side of her husband. The daughter's husband is kneeling in front of her, his arm outstretched towards his daughter who is planting a plant her brother waters with a watering can. The sculpture represents three generations.

Leaves are spread among the apples, many inscribed with the names of churches.

My apple in memory of friends who died of AIDS is in a branch on the right-hand side of the tree.

Hugh's apple is in the center of the tree, at eye level, for the entire world to see.

After a prolonged recovery from a hip fracture, the Rev. Robert W. Wood died on August 19, 2018. He is buried beside Hugh at the New Hampshire State Veterans Cemetery.

Acknowledgments

I owe much gratitude to my chosen family: Roanne Robey, Laura Cassidento, Tom Eck, Victoria Wallins, Jennifer, Stacey and Abe Tanner, with whom I discover *joy in the morning*.

About the Author

Steven Law holds degrees from Campbell University and Colgate Rochester Crozer Divinity School, where his focus was on Christian ethics and social policy. As an ordained pastor, he served rural and urban churches before studying creative writing with C. Michael Curtis, former editor at *The Atlantic Monthly*. He shared forty-five bliss-filled years with Dr. William "Donald" Stroud, with whom he created Découvert Fine Art, an art gallery specializing in European Master drawings. He is founder and president of the Law Stroud Foundation, and lives in Rockport, Massachusetts.